DOWN, BUT NOT OUT

A Study of Divorce and Remarriage in Light of God's Healing Grace

by

Al Maxey

PublishAmerica
Baltimore

ISBN: 1-4137-8993-5
PUBLISHED BY PUBLISHAMERICA, LLLP
www.publishamerica.com
Baltimore

Printed in the United States of America

For *Shelly*,
my wife, lover, best friend,
and "fellow heir of the grace of life,"
with whom I have truly experienced
the *Ideal*

David,

I Love you and
am so proud of you!

Dad

Foreword

Another book on divorce and remarriage? *Yes*, and this one we all need to read and study. It is not just another book on the subject; a rehash of what has already been said. This is no slanted, narrow-scope treatment. This one puts the matter in the context of the entire Bible and of history! Each Old Testament book is summarized separately and a perspective is drawn from each by sound exegesis. The New Testament text is treated with a thoroughness that is rare and an objectivity that is refreshing. For those willing to study patiently and fully, this book will turn on a number of lights to illuminate the field. It is very much textual and contextual.

Note the title: *Down, But Not Out*. This reflects the fact that its theme is the concept of redemption by grace, the biblical idea of forgiveness and new beginnings for fallen people. Al Maxey accepts this divine fundamental, that God's grace is the answer to all sin problems, and that makes his message much more than an exegetical analysis. It is additionally a message of hope and understanding for people whose world has caved in.

Obviously, Al put his heart into this effort. The research is extensive and excellent. It is a rich source of information and should be a prominent part of any Christian's library. But it is more than that. It is also an uplifting work that represents the love of a caring Christian for his fellow travelers who are suffering through traumatic experiences.

Take your time and enjoy each section of this book as you read. The information is good, the analysis accurate, and the conclusions scriptural. Most importantly, it points you to your Savior, who paid the price that you might have a whole new life, and to His view of your situation.

"For God sent not His Son into
the world to condemn the world,
but that the world, through Him,
might be saved." — John 3:17

Olan Hicks
Author & Lecturer
Searcy, Arkansas

Preface

Our world abounds with the walking wounded. Battered, bruised, and bloodied from the encounter with the circumstances of their existence, they strive to move on with their lives, often with shattered dreams and diminished hope. Daily we are surrounded by a host of hurting men, women and young people, and, sadly, we are often completely oblivious to their pain.

One of the most traumatic events of life is without question the breakdown of a marital relationship. It is emotionally, physically, and spiritually devastating; a crushing blow that leaves its victims knocked to the ground, figuratively speaking. Some, indeed, feel unwilling or unable to get back up and re-enter their journey through life. For them the knock*down* blow of divorce has also become a knock*out* blow.

In counseling with the victim of one such marital breakdown, it was revealed that on many occasions he felt so battered by his circumstances in life that he was unsure he could continue on. In time, however, he began to heal. The bright, warming sunshine broke through the gloom encompassing him, and hope for a new day began to dawn in his heart. As his final counseling session ended, his parting remark to me was, "You know, life sure did knock me down for a while, but thanks to God and some of His people it didn't knock me out!"

Some statisticians indicate that divorce is increasing at a rate unprecedented in recorded history. Hardly a nation on earth is left unaffected by this growing plague. That's a lot of hurting people!

Something must be done, not only to prevent these tragic marital breakdowns, but also to provide healing for those involved. It is with the goal of contributing to this process that this book is humbly submitted. It is further offered with the firm conviction that only by a clear perception and promotion of divine principles will this prevention and healing ever truly be realized.

Ours is a world in desperate need of divine guidance with regard to marital relationships. Perhaps no subject has elicited such confusion among both religious and secular scholars as that of how to deal effectively with situations arising out of marriage, divorce and remarriage. One scholar even suggested that in his opinion God had given no clear teaching on the issue whatsoever. Mankind, one would almost think, had been left to muddle through life with no guidance from their Creator.

This study will attempt to demonstrate that this is not the case. God, in His written revelation, speaks clearly and thoroughly to this topic. Although that message has been largely ignored by mankind, or altered to accommodate various religious or theological biases, it can still be heard by those willing to listen.

In this present work an effort has been made to present the divine message as simply and succinctly as possible, for if ever a proclamation of hope and healing needed to be presented, it is now. Those who are suffering the trauma of divorce and the stigma frequently associated with remarriage truly are in need of a revitalizing message of grace.

With a proper understanding of the teachings of our God, perhaps more will be enabled to exclaim, "We are hard pressed on every side, but not crushed; perplexed, but not in despair; persecuted, but not abandoned; struck down, but not destroyed" [2 Corinthians 4:8-9].

To all of those fellow life-travelers who are down, but not yet out, this study of God's inspired revelation is humbly submitted. May it help facilitate your ultimate healing at the hands of a loving and merciful God.

Introduction: The IDEAL

When the Lord God had brought to completion the formation of His vast physical universe, He then created a man "from the dust of the ground and breathed into his nostrils the breath of life, and the man became a living being" [Genesis 2:7]. This newly created man, Adam, was placed within a beautiful garden which God had prepared in the east at a site known as Eden.

At first appearance everything seemed to be perfect. Adam lived in paradise, surrounded by the marvelous wonders of God's creation. The earth was at peace with itself and with its God. What more could be desired? But, God realized that His creative work was not yet completed; something was missing: a vital element that would bring that which was good to perfection. Adam needed a life-companion. The Creator observed, "It is not good for the man to be alone. I will make a helper suitable for him" [vs. 18].

An extensive search was made through the various life-forms which God had created prior to man, but "no suitable helper was found" [vs. 20]. God wanted man to clearly perceive that a compatible mate could not be obtained from any species other than his own. Therefore, the Lord fashioned from the man himself a suitable life-companion, a female of his species, and presented her to him. Adam then observed, in a spirit of appreciation and awe, "This is now bone of my bones and flesh of my flesh; she shall be called 'woman,' for she was taken out of man" [vs. 23].

What we observe here in the very beginning of mankind's existence upon this earth is the eternal, infallible design of the Creator. It is not good for man to be alone. Personal fulfillment is only truly found in an abiding, intimate relationship with a suitable companion. Although the new world abounded with a wide variety of life-forms, none fulfilled the need of man. The intent of our Creator was for woman to be the life-companion of man. "Male and female He created them" [Genesis 1:27], and upon this design He stamped His seal of approval: "God saw all that He had made, and it was very good" [vs. 31].

The IDEAL of God has always been that man and woman would join together in an intimate relationship with one another. God made them "suitable" mates; only they could properly and fully satisfy the needs of the other. Had such fulfillment been possible or desirable from a man-beast or man-man relationship, the Creator would have so designed it. This He determined not to do. The "natural relations" [Romans 1:26-27] of a male with a female is God's design; His IDEAL.

In keeping with such, "God blessed them and said to them, 'Be fruitful and increase in number'" [Genesis 1:28]. This may well be regarded as mankind's first marriage ceremony, with the Lord God Himself officiating. A divine blessing was pronounced upon this man and woman, and they were entrusted with the privilege and responsibility of bearing children through their union. "A man will leave his father and mother and be united to his wife, and they will become one flesh. The man and his wife were both naked, and they felt no shame" [Genesis 2:24-25].

The beauty and innocence of this original design has been brutally twisted and tarnished down through the ages by the numerous abuses and perversions fallen men have inflicted upon it. The natural union of man with woman is being increasingly exchanged for unions which can only be deemed unnatural. The sacred is being cast off in favor of the profane. That which is holy is being trampled underfoot in a senseless quest for immediate, though transient, self-gratification. Intimate relationships, which God designed to be permanent, are being defiled and destroyed by selfish pursuits.

The divine design of our Creator, His IDEAL with regard to the man-woman relationship, is being largely forgotten. Solemn covenants formed between couples in the presence of their God are being broken with little if any remorse. Men and women are desperately seeking out companionship and relationships in almost every conceivable direction except the one originally given by God. In their quest they are overlooking the obvious: It is only in the IDEAL that one truly finds the beauty and depth of fulfillment our Creator intended for mankind.

Throughout the Scriptures, when the Lord confronts the trauma of marital abuse and breakdown, He rarely fails to direct our focus back toward His original intent; His divine design; His IDEAL. For example, the prophet Malachi, prior to stating the Lord's hatred of divorce, called the couples in crisis to remember that the Creator had made them to be one flesh and to recall the beauty of this design [Malachi 2:10-16]. Jesus, while responding to the questions concerning divorce, also directed the hearts and minds of the crowds back to the very beginning. "'Haven't you read,' He replied, 'that at the beginning the Creator "made them male and female," and said, "For this reason a man will leave his father and mother and be united to his wife, and the two will become one flesh?" Therefore what God has joined together, let man not separate'" [Matthew 19:4-6].

Both Jesus and Malachi, when dealing with the problems associated with marital breakdown, realized the importance of lifting high God's original intent for His creation so that they might all appreciate its logic and beauty. Only with an awareness of the Creator's IDEAL could men truly perceive just how far from it they had fallen.

This study will examine in some depth what the inspired Scriptures reveal concerning man's long and painful fall from the IDEAL with regard to marital relationships. Both the consequences of this decline, and God's continued efforts to set mankind back on the pathway toward His original intent, will be highlighted. However, before either can be meaningfully discussed, one must first understand exactly what it is that one has failed to achieve when a marriage ends.

What is the original intent and design of our Creator? As has already been noticed, it is first of all, by God's design, a male-female relationship, and none other. It is a God-ordained event in which a man and woman are joined together in a covenant relationship, thus becoming "one flesh." The apostle Paul writes that marriage is a state created by God, one that is good and not to be rejected, but rather received with thanksgiving in our hearts [1 Timothy 4:3-4]. It is a union blessed by God, designed to be permanent, and not to be dissolved.

The Creator's IDEAL is: one man for one woman for life.

In the beginning, when the Lord formed Eve from out of the very body of Adam, it was never His desire that the two be separate or independent of one another. The very manner of woman's creation, as well as the intricacies of her physical design, clearly indicate the interdependence of man and woman. They were designed to form an intimate union and to rely heavily upon the various strengths and abilities of the other. They were created to find their fulfillment in togetherness. "Woman is not independent of man, nor is man independent of woman. For as woman came from man, so also man is born of woman. But everything comes from God" [1 Corinthians 11:11-12]. God's IDEAL is achieved when the two become one, when they share their lives, when the strengths of one compensate for the weaknesses of the other, and when they each give themselves fully to meeting the needs of the other. Such can only be achieved through union, not separation.

An integral part of this union of male and female is sexual intimacy. Initially, "the man and his wife were both naked, and they felt no shame" [Genesis 2:25]. This blessed state of blissful innocence is hardly characteristic, however, of many of the sexual escapades of fallen man down through the ages. Having forgotten the boundaries within which God has given the privilege of sexual union, "perverse" and "shameful" become far more appropriate depictions of their practice. Although highly scorned as "out-dated" and "old-fashioned" in most permissive societies, sexual expression is restricted by the Creator's design to the marriage bed. "Marriage should be honored by all, and the marriage bed kept pure, for God will judge the adulterer and all the sexually immoral" [Hebrews 13:4]. Having lost sight of this IDEAL of acceptable sexual expression, mankind has inflicted upon itself a host of tragic consequences.

Ideally, the marriage relationship is also to be characterized by emotional nurturing. The apostle Paul, in his epistle to the Ephesians, has penned one of the most moving testimonies to God's IDEAL for marriage found anywhere in the inspired writings [Ephesians 5:22-33]. Consistent with the examples of Jesus and Malachi, he directs the hearts and minds of his readers back to the Genesis account and God's original intent for the marital relationship [vs. 31]. This apostle to the nations further likens marriage to the relationship between Jesus Christ and the church, thus emphasizing anew the sacredness and preciousness of the union between a man and a woman.

"Husbands, love your wives, just as Christ loved the church and gave Himself up for her" [vs. 25]. "In this same way, husbands ought to love their wives as their own bodies. He who loves his wife loves himself. After all, no one ever hated his own body, but he feeds and cares for it, just as Christ does the church" [vs. 28-29]. "Each one of you also must love his wife as he loves himself, and the wife must respect her husband" [vs. 33]. IDEAL marriage consists of mutual love, nurturing, and respect. Without these active qualities any union is on the pathway to disunion.

Note carefully the words of the following biblical marital pledge: "I will betroth you to me forever; I will betroth you in righteousness and justice, in love and compassion. I will betroth you in faithfulness" [Hosea 2:19-20]. These marvelous marriage vows give us additional insight into God's design for this most blessed of interpersonal relationships. It is a forever union of a man and woman, characterized by two hearts focused as one. The focus is upon the other; the vision is of love. It is a walk together through life in righteousness before God, and in faithfulness to one another. It is a compassionate interweaving of two lives into a caring, nurturing whole.

One must not fail to include in any discussion of God's design for marriage the quality of mutual faithfulness to the Lord. Paul clearly warns the people of God not to be "yoked together with unbelievers" [2 Corinthians 6:14]. Although this injunction can validly be applied to various situations in the life of a believer, this in no way discounts or diminishes the marriage relationship as one of those situational applications. A spiritually mixed marriage has within it the seeds of its own destruction. It is a rare couple indeed who has not reaped a harvest of struggle and sorrow over such a union. Often the point is reached when the unbeliever will no longer tolerate the faith of the believing spouse, and will depart, thus terminating the marriage. Paul addresses this very issue in his first epistle to the saints in Corinth. Ideally, husbands and wives will share a common faith, and will work together to achieve the goal of life everlasting. "Husbands, in the same way be considerate as you live with your wives, and treat them with respect as the weaker partner and as heirs with you of the gracious gift of life, so that nothing will hinder your prayers" [1 Peter 3:7].

As one reads through the Scriptures, the IDEAL can be clearly and frequently detected. The Lord God, through His inspired writers, repeatedly holds it before us lest we lose sight of His glorious goal. It is found throughout the laws of Moses; it is immortalized in the glowing tribute to the wife of noble character in Proverbs 31; it is encountered again in the Song of Solomon, a moving love poem overflowing with heartfelt expressions of mutual adoration and devotion. The divine design is discerned in the depth of God's own commitment to His bride Israel, and is perhaps epitomized in the sacrificial love of His Son Jesus for His blood-bought bride the church.

Throughout the course of this study the reader will encounter time and again the concept of God's IDEAL. It has been capitalized throughout this study for the specific purpose of attracting one's attention to it. The eternal design of our Creator for marriage is so vital to our physical, emotional and spiritual well-being that we must never lose sight of it. It must be ever kept before our view. An appreciation of what our God has created for us to achieve will perhaps make us that much more aware of the tragedy of failing to achieve it. Perhaps, additionally, with that awareness will come reassessment of our lives, and recommitment to His IDEAL. This reflective examination of Scripture will conclude by seeking to provide practical, relevant advice designed to facilitate the healing that is so desperately needed by those who have experienced the trauma of marital breakdown.

As we step forward into this deliberation, and as we continue our journey through life, may we never lose sight of the fact that our marvelous Maker desires us to be happy in our interpersonal relationships. Indeed, we are divinely designed to delight in one another. The eternal IDEAL is attainable and maintainable, if we will keep it ever before us and if we will follow the pathway to its acquisition which God has so graciously provided.

Chapter 1
The Law of Moses

Exodus

For hundreds of years the people of Israel had suffered increasing oppression at the hands of the Egyptians, in whose land they dwelt as slaves. Their agonizing cries for relief had ascended to the throne room of God, and in compassion He responded to their need. A deliverer was raised up in the form of a man named Moses, who was able, through a series of remarkable events, to lead them out of their bondage.

Three months later we discover this newly freed people encamped in the Wilderness of Sinai at the base of a mountain bearing the same name. It was at this time, upon Mt. Sinai, that God began to discuss with Moses His plans for the people assembled on the plains below. "This is what you are to say to the house of Jacob and what you are to tell the people of Israel: 'You yourselves have seen what I did to Egypt, and how I carried you on eagles' wings and brought you to Myself. Now if you obey Me fully and keep My covenant, then out of all nations you will be My treasured possession. Although the whole earth is Mine, you will be for Me a kingdom of priests and a holy nation.' These are the words you are to speak to the Israelites" [Exodus 19:3-6].

Moses returned to the people and relayed the words of the Lord to them. One can only imagine the sense of excitement and expectation that must have run through the crowd upon hearing God's prospects for their future. As one they responded, "We will do everything the Lord has said" [vs. 8]. This response was relayed by Moses back to God, Who then informed His chosen deliverer to have the people prepare themselves for an audience with their Lord. They were to wash themselves and their clothes, they were to "abstain from sexual relations" [vs. 15], and they were to prepare themselves in heart, mind

17

and body for that encounter. In three days time God would come before them.

On the morning of the third day, with the people assembled in awed anticipation, the God of Abraham, Isaac and Jacob descended in glory upon Mt. Sinai. A thick cloud covered the mountain. Thunder and lightening, accompanied by "a very loud trumpet blast" [vs. 16], provided a stunning audio-visual display. "Mount Sinai was covered with smoke, because the Lord descended on it in fire. The smoke billowed up from it like smoke from a furnace, the whole mountain trembled violently, and the sound of the trumpet grew louder and louder" [vs. 18-19]. So overwhelmed were the people of Israel that "everyone in the camp trembled" [vs. 16]. "Then Moses led the people out of the camp to meet with God, and they stood at the foot of the mountain" [vs. 17].

With His chosen people assembled before Him, God entered into a solemn covenant with them. They would be His people, and He would be their God. This would be a special, spiritual relationship very much like a marriage between a man and woman; indeed, it would often be referred to as such in the Scriptures. This was the wedding day of Almighty God to His bride Israel; a moment of deep spiritual significance that forms a foundation for the understanding of much of what will follow in the course of this study.

It is also significant to note that it was at this time that God chose to impart to Moses the details of His expectations for this new relationship. A series of ten commandments were conveyed to His bride which deal in large part with how to solidify relationships with both God and one's fellow man.

The first of these commands [Exodus 20:3-6] indicates that God desired a monogamous relationship with His new bride. They were to have no other gods (husbands) besides Him, "for I, the Lord your God, am a jealous God" [vs. 5]. This principle was also to be observed in their own personal marriage relationships. "You shall not commit adultery" [vs. 14]; "you shall not covet your neighbor's wife" [vs. 17]. Through these commands God was re-emphasizing the IDEAL: one man for one woman for life. It was to be a relationship of total commitment, intense devotion and complete faithfulness on the part of both parties for the duration of their lives. These covenant relationships are viewed by God as sacred. They are entered into solemnly, and are to be taken seriously.

Along with the Ten Commandments, God delivered to Moses several additional "laws you are to set before them" [Exodus 21:1]. They begin with principles and laws detailing God's will in the matter of the treatment of Hebrew slaves.

It was not uncommon in the ancient world for a nation to capture and enslave individuals from a neighboring or enemy nation. Even the people of Israel engaged in this practice. It was also not uncommon to find individuals from among one's own people who chose, for various reasons, to become indentured laborers. Through a series of special laws, God instructed His people that servants acquired from among their own brethren were to be shown special consideration. In no way were they to be treated as one might be prone to treat a captured enemy. Regardless of their social or economic status, and regardless of the circumstances that brought them to the point of indentured labor, they were first and foremost brethren, and were to be treated as such.

"If you buy a Hebrew servant, he is to serve you for six years. But in the seventh year, he shall go free, without paying anything" [vs. 2]. If this man had a wife when he entered the service of another, she must also be allowed to go free with him [vs. 3]. The wife was not to be regarded as the property of the master. The sacred relationship between husband and wife was to be honored; it could not be severed by the master capriciously.

If, however, "his master gives him a wife and she bears him sons or daughters, the woman and her children shall belong to her master, and only the man shall go free" [vs. 4]. The woman given to this servant as a wife was already in the possession of the master, therefore even though this Hebrew servant should choose to accept his own freedom at the end of six years of indentured service, the woman was not thereby freed, nor were any children they may have had during their marriage. Admittedly, this is difficult for us, with societal conditions and standards radically different from those of that time and place, to fully

19

comprehend, or even to accept. However, it must be noted that, regardless of our modern perceptions, these were the prevailing conditions under which these ancient peoples lived their lives. This was their reality.

Although the situation described above certainly conveys an appearance of despair for the Hebrew servant and his family, it was not as hopeless as one might initially imagine. The fact that the master had the legal "right of ownership" to the wife and children, did not necessarily demand that he was under compulsion to exercise that right. If this master was a kind and compassionate man, as God expected, he may well have been moved to free the wife and children together with their husband and father. "Masters, provide your slaves with what is right and fair, because you know that you also have a Master in heaven" [Colossians 4:1].

Although the law God delivered to Moses with regard to the acquired families of indentured servants did serve a legitimate purpose (it prevented the unscrupulous from using marriage as a tool for taking away the servants of another, for example), it also served, on another level, as a test of the master's character. Just how loving, kind and compassionate was he willing to be toward one of his own brethren who had genuinely entered into a covenant of marriage with another of his servants? Whether this master exercised his legal rights, or whether he chose to forfeit them for the good of another, would speak volumes about the condition of his heart. The apostle Paul used a similar approach, appealing to one's spiritual side, when writing to Philemon about his runaway slave, now a brother-in-Christ, Onesimus, "so that your goodness should not be as it were by compulsion, but of your own free will" [Philemon 14]. Just how much was one willing to relinquish for the good of another? To a degree, this was the challenge facing the master as he contemplated his brother in need in light of this law from God.

But, what if the master was not a merciful and compassionate man? Or, what if he was simply not in a position economically to release the man's family at that particular time. If he chose to exercise his legal rights as a master and retain the wife and children, what recourse did this servant have who had now completed his six years of service? At this point, the challenge previously posed to the master comes before the servant: how much are *you* willing to relinquish?! If the servant was willing to give up his freedom, and to give himself into service to this master for life, he would be allowed by law to keep his wife and children [vs. 5-6].

This law now becomes a test of the heart of the servant. How deeply was he committed to his relationship with his wife and children? How seriously did he take that covenant? Enough to give up his freedom for life to maintain that relationship?! It should be noted that if this servant was the type of man who was merely interested in a short-term relationship, or who was seeking a "legal loophole" to terminate his relationship, he certainly had an opportunity here to display that lack of character. Some have even been so daring as to accuse God of providing an avenue whereby one could legally abandon his wife and children. However, properly perceived, this law was an opportunity to bring out the *best* in a man, not the worst. It was a call to rise above one's own selfish interests; a call to self-sacrifice; a call to consider others first. Both men, first the master and then the slave, were presented with an opportunity to forfeit something to achieve a greater good. The former was challenged to forfeit possessions, the latter to forfeit freedom. The result in either case was the preservation of the covenant relationship of marriage between a man and his wife. The question being posed to all parties in this situation was this: just how much are you personally willing to sacrifice to assure that God's IDEAL is achieved? No, God was *not* cheapening the marriage covenant here, as some imply. He was demonstrating it's incalculable value!

As one continues to examine the first eleven verses of Exodus 21, in which various laws concerning Hebrew slaves are presented, additional challenges to the preservation of the covenant of marriage are detected.

Most biblical scholars, after pondering the statement in verse 9, interpret it as a reference to a master taking a particular female slave, who had been previously sold to him, and giving her to his own son as his wife. A few suggest that the intent of the passage is that the master himself takes the female slave as a wife, which is certainly a possible meaning. In either case, there is little doubt left in the minds of the readers that a state of marriage has been entered into.

If, however, the one who takes this female slave as his wife "marries another woman" [vs. 10], his responsibilities to the former are not thereby terminated. Because he has decided, for whatever reason, to end the relationship, does not relieve him of his obligations to this woman with whom he previously entered into a covenant of marriage.

Spouses can at times be extremely hardhearted and cruel toward one another. This is true today, and it was especially true then. Abandoning a wife in that day and age, particularly if that woman was a slave and had brought nothing into the relationship, was tantamount to a death sentence. She was "used goods," "discarded property," and in general scorned, despised and rejected by society. Left to fend for herself with little or no resources, her future was very bleak.

Due to the hardness of heart of some of His people, God made provision in His law for the care of these women who had been cruelly rejected by their husbands. "If he marries another woman, he must not deprive the first one of her food, clothing and marital rights. If he does not provide her with these three things, she is to go free, without any payment of money" [vs. 10-11]. If this man absolutely refused to meet his obligations to this woman, even though he had been commanded by God to do so, then at the very least she was to be given her freedom from servitude, and this was to be done without any penalty against her. She was not to be returned to the ranks of the other slaves. Because of his cruelty toward her, she had at least gained her complete freedom and was no longer to be regarded or treated as a slave. She was free.

It is important not to draw more from this passage than is clearly being taught. For example, some have suggested that because God fashioned laws providing for the care of "put away" women that this in some way implies His *approval* of the "putting away" process. Such reasoning is hardly worthy of the name. Providing for the relief of victims in no way suggests approval of the victimizers or of their crimes. When the "good Samaritan" provided care for the victim he found near death upon the road between Jerusalem and Jericho [Luke

10], his compassionate actions could in no way be construed as approval of either the crimes of robbery and assault or of the perpetrators themselves. So it is with God and the laws He has issued to help alleviate the pain of those who have been victimized by the cruelties of others.

By casting off the slave woman so as to join himself to another, God's IDEAL had been battered and cast by the wayside, as had the former wife. Through no fault of the slave woman, she found herself "put away." Although her husband was obligated by law to make concessions to her, the stigma of her situation would nevertheless follow with her. Through his hardheartedness, she had been damaged, and she would have to live with the scars of those wounds for the rest of her life. Although this law from God was designed to relieve her of some of that burden, it certainly could not eradicate it completely. She had been traumatized; there would always be scars.

God's primary concern here was for the woman, not the man. The Lord was addressing the age old issue of victim's rights. The fact that He *recognized* the severing of this marriage covenant is in no way to be interpreted as His *approval* of it. It was sin. Sin committed by the man against the woman. This divine perception is foundational and fundamental for an understanding of the later teachings of God's Son with regard to similar assaults against the Father's IDEAL, and who must ultimately bear the guilt for the destruction of the marital relationship.

Leviticus

As the search through the Pentateuch continues, all in an effort to more fully understand the will of our God with regard to marital relationships gone awry, we quickly come upon Leviticus 21, in which we find a host of regulations dealing with God's priests. The members of the priesthood were ideally to be examples of holy living to the people of God. In many ways they were required to be "a cut above the rest." As the religious and spiritual leaders of the people of Israel, they were compelled to set a standard in their lives that was worthy of imitation. "They must be holy to their God and must not profane the name of their God ... they are to be holy" [vs. 6].

As a part of this visible display of holiness before the people, these priests were given some very specific regulations to observe with regard to marriage. "They must not marry women defiled by prostitution or divorced from their husbands, because priests are holy to their God" [vs. 7]. "The woman he marries must be a virgin. He must not marry a widow, a divorced woman, or a woman defiled by prostitution, but only a virgin from his own people, so he will not defile his offspring among his people. I am the Lord, who sets him apart as holy" [vs. 13-15]. The regulation concerning widows is given further clarification in Ezekiel 44:22-23. "They must not marry widows or divorced women; they may marry only virgins of Israelite descent or widows of priests. They are to teach My people the difference between the holy and the common and show them how to distinguish between the unclean and the clean."

It should be noted that God has always required an extra measure of devotion and commitment from those called to lead His people. They are divinely challenged to be living examples of the IDEAL in every area of life. Even in the church, His spiritual leaders are to be "examples to the flock" [1 Peter 5:3]. They have been called to a high standard of holiness in both attitude and action that will shine forth as a beacon directing others to godly living. They are to be the "husband of but one wife" [1 Timothy 3:2,12; Titus 1:6], thus exemplifying God's IDEAL for marriage: one man for one woman for life!

The marital relationships of God's leaders were, and still are, to be living proof that the IDEAL is indeed attainable, and not only attainable, but also preferable to the standards established and practiced by the world. If the people of God can visibly witness the IDEAL in practice in the daily lives of their spiritual leaders, not only are they provided with an objective source of reference for the directing of their own lives, but in addition they are provided with the incentive to try and recreate these same success stories they behold in their guides. "Consider the outcome of their way of life and imitate their faith" [Hebrews 13:7].

Lest some misunderstand the teaching of God as it pertains to the marital restrictions of the Levitical priesthood, it should be stressed that He is not condemning, nor labeling as unclean or unworthy of His love, those who find themselves either widowed or divorced. In all the above passages from the Law the only woman God declares "defiled" is the prostitute. It has been suggested that because God forbids His priests to marry a divorced woman, He is thereby displaying His disapproval and condemnation of her. If this were indeed a logical assumption from the text, then would it not also logically apply to the widow? However, we know from numerous passages throughout the Scriptures that God has a special place in His heart for those who have been widowed. As will soon be amply displayed, God's vast resources of love and compassion *also* extend to those who find themselves the victims of a broken covenant relationship with a spouse.

In Leviticus 22:13 the discussion of regulations for priests continues, but in this passage the focus shifts from the priest to his children. "But if a priest's daughter becomes a widow or is divorced, yet has no children, and she returns to live in her father's house as in her youth, she may eat of her father's food. No unauthorized person, however, may eat any of it." Although on the surface it may not appear to be, this is nevertheless an extremely important passage. In it we begin to see a little more clearly God's appraisal of those who have experienced a divorce.

There is little question as to how God views divorce itself. "'I hate divorce,' says the Lord God of Israel" [Malachi 2:16]. Although His feelings against the *state* of divorce are intense, those same feelings of loathing and disgust do not carry over to the *victims* of this tragedy. This fact is discovered very quickly when a comparison is made between the Leviticus 22:13 passage and a couple of other key statements in the Pentateuch.

As has already been noted in the above Scripture, no unauthorized person was permitted to eat of the priest's food. Many of the food items which were offered up unto God in the form of various sacrifices were authorized by God to be used as a source of food for the priests. This was considered their rightful portion. Although this is pointed out repeatedly in the Law, notice especially the following: "But you and your sons and your daughters may eat the breast that was waved and the thigh that was presented. Eat them in a ceremonially clean place; they have been given to you and your children as your share of the Israelites' fellowship offerings" [Leviticus 10:14].

Therefore, the priests of God, along with their families, were authorized to eat of the foods offered up to God by the people of Israel. With this fact in mind, consider the following: "This also is yours: whatever is set aside from the gifts of all the wave offerings of the Israelites. I give this to you and your sons and daughters as your regular share. Everyone in your household who is ceremonially clean may eat it" [Numbers 18:11]. Note carefully this last declaration of God! Those in the household of the priest who are regarded as *clean* in the sight of God may eat of the priest's food; food which had previously been offered in sacrifice to God!

By putting all of this information together, we arrive at a stunning picture of God's grace and acceptance as perceived in Leviticus 22:13. How does God view the divorced daughter of the priest in that passage? She is CLEAN! How does one know that? God clearly states, "She may eat of her father's food," a privilege extended *only* to those God regards as being clean. Nothing is said about who was to blame for this divorce, the husband or the wife, or if perhaps both may have contributed to the destruction of the relationship; nothing is mentioned about guilty or innocent parties; nothing is stated about potential reconciliation. It is a rather general, nonspecific statement covering all daughters of all priests who might find themselves put away by a spouse. *They are clean.*

How tragic and unjustified it is that far too many in the religious world down through the ages have characterized the divorced as being defiled, unclean, or in some way spiritually inferior. In a spirit of great "generosity," and with a show of unparalleled "grace," some might cautiously, and even reluctantly, grant them admittance into God's kingdom. However, they are often then quickly relegated to the back ranks; the less visible areas of service; for, after all, they are "unclean." Although such may indeed be the response of some *men*, it should be noted that it is not the response of *God*. His grace is limitless; His acceptance far-reaching. With a declaration of "Thou art CLEAN," He has granted the divorced daughters of the priests full and unhindered access to the table where His offerings are being consumed by His holy ones. This is the view from Heaven. Should the view of man be any less grace-centered?

Yes, God hates divorce. But, God also realizes that it *does* happen, sometimes in the best of families, and sometimes to the best of people. Bad things *do*, on occasion, happen to good people. When life strikes out with a knockdown blow, God graciously provides the resources enabling one to rise again and proceed on with life. How frightening the thought should be to each one of us that we might actually be found guilty of invalidating God's merciful provision to a soul in distress by shunning and regarding as unclean those whom God Himself has not.

Numbers

As one moves deeper into the Pentateuch in search of God's eternal teaching on this most vital subject, one soon encounters Numbers 30. In this passage the focus shifts to the Law of Vows. Both the validity of one's vows, and the means whereby a vow may be nullified, are discussed in some depth. This law states, "Any vow or obligation taken by a widow or divorced woman will be binding on her" [vs. 9]. The verses preceding and succeeding this statement indicate that a woman who is under the authority of either a father or husband may have her vows annulled by them if they deem their daughter's vows or wife's vows to be inappropriate. If these vows have been annulled by those in authority over her, she is no longer obligated before God to fulfill them.

In the case of a woman who is widowed or divorced, however, there is no longer a figure of authority over her. Having become married, she was removed from the authority of her father, and having become widowed or divorced, she was removed from the authority of her husband. Therefore, if she makes a vow, or obligates herself in some way, this shall be binding upon her. There is no longer any recognized male authority figure in her life who has the legal right to free her from these vows.

Again, one should exercise great caution in the interpretation of such passages lest more be assumed than the Lord is specifically conveying. This is not a passage designed to condemn those who are divorced, any more than it is designed to condemn those who are widowed. It merely states an important fact with respect to the vows of a woman before her God: without a husband, whether that state be due to death or divorce, the responsibilities of a woman with regard to her vows *change*. It was important that these women who found themselves suddenly without husbands be aware of this important change.

One thing which can be logically and necessarily inferred from this passage, however, is that when a woman is divorced from her husband, that husband's authority over her is thereby *terminated*. It is the contention of some in the religious world that God simply does not recognize the reality of a divorce; that the two are in fact still married; that no dissolution of that relationship has actually occurred. After all, did not Jesus say, "What God has joined together, let man not separate" [Matthew 19:6]? Divorce is a willful act of man, it is argued, thus not recognized by God as valid. In His eyes, therefore, they are still joined as one flesh. This is certainly a popular view in some rather fundamentalist circles, but it simply cannot be justified by sound exegesis of Scripture.

It should be noted that Jesus does not say, "What God has joined together, man *cannot* separate." Our Lord nowhere suggests that such severing of marital relationships is *impossible*, rather that they are *unacceptable*. Jesus urged His hearers to seek out a higher goal; to strive for the IDEAL; to refrain from the frivolous fracturing of relationships that was so much in vogue at that time.

It should be obvious, from even a cursory examination of the Numbers 30:9 passage on vows, that God no longer recognized the authority of a man over a woman who found herself divorced from him. That authority had ceased. Why? Because the marriage relationship itself, upon which that authority was based, had ceased. This passage says nothing about guilty or innocent parties, or God's feelings about divorce, it simply recognizes the reality of a covenant relationship which has ended, and speaks to the situation this woman thereby finds herself in with regard to her vows before God.

Deuteronomy

In the fifth and final book of the Pentateuch, Deuteronomy, one encounters several extremely important passages dealing with the subject of marriage, divorce, and remarriage. With the continual drift of His people away from the IDEAL, God was compelled to speak directly to, and make provisions for, their obstinate and rebellious hearts. The Deuteronomy passages are perhaps the most critical in all the Pentateuch, and will be referred to and alluded to throughout the teachings of the New Testament on this subject. Thus, it is vital that they be carefully examined to determine their proper meaning.

The first passage which must be prayerfully evaluated consists of laws regulating one's marriage to a female captive. "When you go to war against your enemies and the Lord your God delivers them into your hands and you take captives, if you notice among the captives a beautiful woman and are attracted to her, you may take her as your wife. Bring her into your home and have her shave her head, trim her nails and put aside the clothes she was wearing when captured. After she has lived in your house and mourned her father and mother for a full month, then you may go to her and be her husband and she shall be your wife" [Deuteronomy 21:10-13]. There can be little doubt that this passage clearly teaches that a state of marriage does indeed exist between the captor and the captive. The phrase "you may go to her" is generally understood to signify the sexual consummation of the marriage. Although the various cultural aspects of this passage may seem strange to us, nevertheless few would argue that this is not a legitimate marital relationship, one which is recognized as such by God.

In time of war it is not uncommon for fighting men to be attracted to young women from among the conquered people. This practice is almost as old as man himself, and has been witnessed in every era and in every corner of the earth. However, it is also a fact that in many cases these attractions are not long-lived. The cultural, religious, and often racial differences soon become increasingly noticeable, and they often become the source of conflict within the relationship. The passionate emotions of war all too soon are replaced by the realities of being "back home" where one's choices soon begin to be questioned. Not a few "war brides" have found themselves abandoned as a result of this re-evaluation process. It is *this* that very likely has taken place within the context of the passage before us. "If you are not pleased with her, let her go wherever she wishes. You must not sell her or treat her as a slave, since you have dishonored her" [vs. 14].

Although no specifics are enumerated which might have led to this decision, the passage presents a husband who has resolved to terminate the marriage relationship. The only motivating factor mentioned is he no longer "delights in her" (*King James Version*); he has lost his "liking for her" (*New American Bible*, St. Joseph edition). For whatever cause, he no longer feels the same intensity of affection as at first. His desire for her has diminished, and he no longer takes any pleasure in her company. Again, no justification is presented in the text for these negative feelings. They simply exist. One can only speculate as to whether the behavior of the wife prompted this ultimate breakdown of relationship, or if the responsibility lies solely at the feet of the husband. From the general tone of the passage one may well assume the latter, although it is a rare case indeed where *both* parties have not contributed in some measure to the ultimate demise of the union.

All speculation as to motivation aside, the fact remains that a marriage has come to a tragic end. This being true, there are now practical matters that must be addressed by law. Since the man's wife was originally a captive of war, and not one of his own people, the temptation might exist to make a profit from the situation by selling her into slavery. Undoubtedly such situations were not that uncommon. Thus, God declares His abhorrence of such a heartless action. The husband was not even to *regard* her as a slave, much less sell her as one. The fact that this woman had been taken from her homeland and family, and was now being cast aside in a strange land, was dishonor and humiliation enough. She was not to be further shamed by being sold to the highest bidder as a piece of property. Such an action God would not tolerate. His law demanded that she be set free, and that she be allowed to go wherever she wished. The husband must at least show her that much respect, and grant to her that degree of dignity.

Through the provisions of this law, God displayed tremendous sensitivity and compassion for the plight of women. Feelings which, one might add, have not diminished in the least with the passage of time. God would not force a man to love and cherish his wife. He does not even force such feelings from mankind for Himself. Such would be a violation of man's free will. God would not even force this man to maintain the marriage relationship with his wife, although God certainly *desired* that he do so. The fact that the husband chose not to, however, clearly demonstrates that he had fallen short of the IDEAL, and "missing the mark" is sin.

One thing God *did* insist upon, however, and clearly demanded in the Law of Moses, was that a woman put away by her husband be treated with as much dignity and respect as was humanly possible in such a difficult situation, if indeed this action against her was through no fault of her own. The trauma she was experiencing was not to be compounded by acts of cruelty and vindictiveness.

It should be clearly understood that God is in no way condoning the actions of the husband, nor is this an indirect authorization of such behavior. Simply because God does not specifically condemn the attitudes and actions of the husband in this passage does not thereby demonstrate His approval of them. Neither does the fact of His provision for the proper treatment of the cast off wife imply His favorable acceptance of the state of divorce. Any time people fail to live up to God's IDEAL, whether it be in marriage or any other area of life, there will always be victims, both innocent and otherwise. When sin occurs, people get hurt. The gracious purpose and provision of the Lord, through the enacting of this law and others like it, was to try and minimize that hurt for those who had been victimized by the breakdown of a marital relationship.

Moving on to the next chapter of the book of Deuteronomy

[chapter 22], there begins a rather lengthy section dealing with various laws on moral conduct relating to marriage. Specific moral violations and their consequences are discussed at some length. Throughout the Pentateuch, and especially within the Law of Moses, God has made it exceedingly clear that He expects the interpersonal relationships of His people to be on a spiritual plane far above that of the pagan world about them. This was particularly true of the marriage relationship between a man and woman, which was to be held in high esteem and never defiled in any way. "Marriage should be honored by all, and the marriage bed kept pure, for God will judge the adulterer and all the sexually immoral" [Hebrews 13:4].

The following excerpt from God's holy Law makes it clear that He is indeed serious about this: "If a man is found sleeping with another man's wife, both the man who slept with her and the woman must die. You must purge the evil from Israel" [Deuteronomy 22:22]. On one occasion, the scribes and Pharisees brought just such a case before Jesus. Dragging before Him a woman caught in the very act of adultery, they said, "In the Law Moses commanded us to stone such women. Now what do You say?" [John 8:5]. What these men failed to state here was that in the Law Moses also commanded the *man* to be stoned as well! Nevertheless, Jesus used this incident to display an attitude of forgiveness and mercy. He also used it to challenge the woman to seek to live up to God's IDEAL in the various areas of her life from that point forward. "Go now and leave your life of sin!" The fact that Jesus refused to condemn her, or authorize her execution, in no way demonstrated His approval of her actions. She had sinned. Under the Law, men and women died without mercy for their sins [Hebrews 10:28]; in Christ Jesus, God extends grace, and with it an opportunity to rise above one's failures.

With the above thoughts on moral conduct in mind, notice the following statement of God's Law: "If a man happens to meet a virgin who is not pledged to be married and rapes her and they are discovered, he shall pay the girl's father fifty shekels of silver. He must marry the girl, for he has violated her. He can never divorce her as long as he lives" [Deuteronomy 22:28-29].

Once again God displays concern and compassion for one who has been victimized by another. A young maiden who had been defiled by a man through a violent act of sexual assault was typically regarded as "spoiled goods." Her desirability as a suitable mate was lessened greatly, which resulted in social and economic harm both to herself and to her family. The man guilty of the rape, therefore, was required to make a form of double restitution. Not only must he pay a penalty to the girl's father, but he was also compelled to marry his victim. Further, due to his violation of her, he could never divorce her. This assured that as long as she lived she would never have to face social or economic deprivation due to his act of aggression against her.

In most societies today it is highly doubtful that a woman would even consider for a moment marrying a man who had raped her. It's virtually unthinkable. However, among the ancient Israelites this was indeed a viable option, especially considering the socio-economic alternatives that would inevitably be faced by this young maiden and her family otherwise. By engaging in cultural comparisons, and the shock to our sensibilities that often comes from such comparative analysis, we face the danger of failing to perceive God's original intent in this provision of law. Operating through the various cultural norms of that day, this was an effective means of assuring victims' rights. This *principle* can be enacted in any time or place; the *methodology*, obviously, is subject to change.

Another aspect of moral conduct within interpersonal relationships that God addressed in the Law revealed unto His people through Moses is found in Deuteronomy 22:13-21. If a man could convincingly prove that his wife was not a virgin when he married her, he was legally entitled to a divorce. In fact, he could even have her executed, if he so desired.

Some disreputable men were apparently using this law as a means whereby they might bring their marriages to an end in a manner "acceptable" before God and man. Thus, bringing false charges against their wives, accusing them of not having been virgins at the time of their marriage, they demanded that the union be declared legally dissolved. Undoubtedly, many women were publicly shamed and disgraced, to say nothing of abandoned, by this unscrupulous and heartless practice.

Therefore, God made the following provision of Law: If the charges of the husband could be proven to be false, "the elders shall take the man and punish him. They shall fine him a hundred shekels of silver and give them to the girl's father, because this man has given an Israelite virgin a bad name. She shall continue to be his wife; he must not divorce her as long as he lives" [vs. 18-19]. God once again forbids the option of divorce for life. In this case it is for bringing shame upon the good name of a fellow Israelite and her family, a wrong which could prove devastating if not disproved. The callous, conniving husband is not only given a stiff fine, but incurs as an additional penalty the life-long responsibility of providing for his wife. This was to be an obligation from which he could only be released by death, and one which he should have been willing to fulfill all along without the need for the intervention of law.

In all the situations discussed in Deuteronomy 22, of which the above are merely a selective sampling, the emphasis is consistently upon the necessity of developing and maintaining godly interpersonal relationships, and the consequences which must be suffered when this does not occur. In each of these passages God's IDEAL is ever elevated as the standard by which God's people are to live, and in every circumstance of life where that standard is not sought after, people suffer. In most of these cases, the scars of the wounded are worn for the remainder of their lives. Failing to achieve the IDEAL is devastating and destructive, and throughout His Law God continually sought to impress that fact upon His people.

The final passage in the Pentateuch which deals specifically with divorce and remarriage is perhaps the most frequently quoted of them all. Our understanding of the teachings of both Jesus and Paul with reference to this subject would certainly be incomplete without it. Thus, it is imperative that one fully appreciate the significance of this Scripture — Deuteronomy 24:1-4 — before endeavoring to interpret the teachings of the New Testament writings.

As a prelude to the examination of this final text in the Law of Moses, one should first take note of the verse which immediately succeeds it; an insightful statement which provides some significant guidance on how to acquire the IDEAL in a newly formed marital relationship. "If a man has recently married, he must not be sent to war or have any other duty laid on him. For one year he is to be free to stay at home and bring happiness to the wife he has married" [vs. 5].

In the early, formative years of a relationship between a husband and wife it is absolutely essential they be together as much as possible. It is at this critical time they begin to form those bonds which will see them through a lifetime of challenges to their covenant with one another. Newlyweds who are separated for extended periods of time are almost certain to face abnormal levels of marital distress and, potentially, disaster.

Many a soldier who married his high school sweetheart and then went off to war found himself devastated by the arrival of a "Dear John" letter. Such letters are a testimony to the wisdom of God's guidance for newlyweds in His Law. It is His will that the first year of marriage, at the very least, be spent in solidifying the relationship between husband and wife, and that no undue burdens or demands be placed upon them during this critical time which might contribute to the breakdown of that sacred union. Once again we see reflected in His Law His great concern that every effort be made to attain and maintain the IDEAL in marriage.

As one considers the first four verses of Deuteronomy 24, however, a situation is encountered which, sadly, falls far short of God's IDEAL. "If a man marries a woman who becomes displeasing to him because he finds something indecent about her, and he writes her a certificate of divorce, gives it to her and sends her from his house, and if after she leaves his house she becomes the wife of another man, and her second husband dislikes her and writes her a certificate of divorce, gives it to her and sends her from his house, or if he dies, then her first husband, who divorced her, is not allowed to marry her again after she has been defiled. That would be detestable in the eyes of the Lord. Do not bring sin upon the land the Lord your God is giving you as an inheritance."

In Deuteronomy 21:14 the phrase "if you are not pleased with her" is given as the motivation for the husband's putting away his wife. A similar statement is found in the present text: "If a man marries a woman who becomes displeasing to him... ." However, an additional qualifier is added that is not found in the previous passage: "...because he finds something indecent about her."

This phrase is variously rendered in the English translations of the Scriptures. Most favor the use of the idea conveyed by "indecency," although "uncleanness" (*King James Version*), "something shameful" (*New English Bible*), and other similar expressions are also found. Perhaps the most specific translation of this passage, and without doubt one of the most interesting, is taken from the Aramaic of the *Peshitta*, in which the text is rendered this way: "Because he has found some evidence of *open prostitution* in her."

This phrase, as it appears in the *Septuagint* (an ancient translation of the Hebrew Scriptures into the Greek language for the benefit of the Greek speaking Jews of the Dispersion; likely produced in the 3rd century B.C., and often quoted by the authors of the New Testament documents), is "aschemon pragma." The first word in the phrase means "shameful, indecent, dishonorable, lewd, unbecoming," and usually carries with it a negative sexual connotation. It appears only once in the New Testament writings, where it is used with reference to the less presentable parts of the human body which must be "treated with special modesty" [1 Corinthians 12:23]. It appears only one other time in the Old Testament documents, where Shechem's rape of Jacob's daughter Dinah is described as "a disgraceful thing" [Genesis 34:7].

The second word in the phrase signifies "a deed; a thing done; a practice, action, transaction, or affair." The statement which appears in Deuteronomy 24:1, therefore, indicates that the husband had discovered in his wife some shameful, indecent, perhaps sexually disgraceful action or practice. This could refer to an adulterous affair, or even, in the extreme, as some suggest, open prostitution. Whatever the actual circumstances may have been, her shameful activities had brought disgrace and destruction in their wake, and the husband made the determination that his only recourse was to issue his wife a certificate of divorce and thus legally terminate their relationship.

Undoubtedly, these same thoughts must have been going through the mind of Joseph when he discovered that Mary was pregnant by one other than himself. He determined that he had no option other than to "divorce her quietly" [Matthew 1:18-19].

In Deuteronomy 24 the husband makes the decision to put away his wife, and thus issues her a "certificate of divorce." This particular certificate is mentioned three times in the pages of the New Testament writings [Matthew 5:31; 19:7; Mark 10:4], and four times in the writings of the Old Testament [Isaiah 50:1 and Jeremiah 3:8 being the other two locations]. It was an official document which gave notice that a covenant of marriage was now and henceforth to be recognized as legally terminated. Neither party was any longer, nor in any way, bound to the other. Both were free, in the eyes of the Law, to engage in new relationships.

As before, it should be stressed that although God permitted the issuing of such certificates, this did not thereby imply His approval of the state of divorce. Anything less than the IDEAL can only be regarded as displeasing in His sight, even though He repeatedly made compassionate provision for those victimized by such tragic occurrences. Divorce was never a part of God's plan for marriage; it holds no place within His IDEAL. It was because of the hardness of the people's hearts toward one another that God "permitted" divorce. This provision served only to prevent further abuse and cruelty toward one's spouse, *not* to grant divine approval [Matthew 19:8]. The Law was made necessary because of sin [1 Timothy 1:9-10]. Had mankind been living righteously before God, the Law would have been unnecessary.

In order to fully understand the intent and significance of Deuteronomy 24:1-4, and how God views divorce and remarriage, it is also important to notice some of the terminology utilized. In this passage the divorced woman is said to become "the *wife* of another man" [vs. 2], who is then referred to as her "second *husband*" [vs. 3]. He too issued her a certificate of divorce, indicating that a legal marriage was being dissolved. The first husband is commanded not to "*marry* her again" [vs. 4]. What is the message here? Is it, as some have suggested, that God does not really recognize divorce? Does this terminology imply that no covenant of marriage was ever broken, and that the first husband is still in fact the only husband, with the second man "living in adultery/sin" with a married woman? *If* such concepts are legitimate biblical doctrines, one would be hard-pressed to demonstrate it from *this* passage.

The second relationship of this divorced woman is clearly and distinctly viewed as being one of "husband" and "wife." If the first marriage was never actually dissolved, then what is to be made of the statement forbidding the first man to marry this woman *again*? It has been theorized that this simply meant that one was not to *renew* his marriage vows in a public ceremony if his wife had been unfaithful to him. This, however, is little more than a feeble attempt to prove an untenable theological position. The text clearly recognizes that one marriage has ended and another has been entered into, which in turn also comes to an end. The second union is viewed as nothing less than a legal covenant of marriage, and the participants are represented as nothing other than husband and wife.

These *provisions* of God's Law in no way suggest He is *pleased* with the tragic failures manifested in the lives of His people. They have failed to achieve the IDEAL, and that grieves Him greatly. These provisions *do* suggest, however, that God is painfully aware of the many circumstances and consequences of their behavior. God is a realist, and He responds to man's needs realistically. Marriages had ended; new marriages had begun; and God addressed Himself to those realities. To maintain that God never recognized the termination of the first union, nor the establishment of the second, is to declare far more than the text itself affirms. Indeed, it is to declare the very opposite.

Another aspect of this particular passage from the Law of Moses that often perplexes the reader is why the first husband was forbidden to remarry his former wife. If she was later divorced by the second husband, or if he died, "then her first husband, who divorced her, is not allowed to marry her again after she has been defiled" [vs. 4]. For him to do so would be "detestable in the eyes of the Lord," or "an abomination," and it would "bring sin upon the land that the Lord your God is giving you as an inheritance" [vs. 4]. For a man to take back as his wife a woman who had been defiled was considered by God an odious act.

This raises the question as to the nature of that which defiled her and rendered her too loathsome for remarriage. Some have postulated that it was the fact that she was married a *second time*. In other words, she was "living in sin," and was thereby defiled. Nowhere, however, is this second union even remotely characterized as "living in sin," or as being an adulterous relationship. The text regards it simply as a marriage. Others have suggested that it was the fact of a *second divorce* that produced her state of defilement. But, this theory is invalidated by the fact that she was regarded as defiled even though she continued married to the second husband until the time of his death.

The most logical explanation as to the nature of that which defiled her can be determined by referring back to the first verse of the text, in which it is revealed that the first husband divorced her because he found "something indecent about her." As noticed earlier, the evidence is strong that she was engaged in sexually inappropriate conduct. A heart filled with immorality, and a conscience seared over and unconcerned about such behavior, would certainly be sufficient to defile one in the sight of one's spouse, society, and Sovereign. It's not inconceivable that such behavior may well have led to her second divorce, or may even have been a contributing factor to the demise of her second husband. Although such is admittedly speculative, it certainly falls within the realm of possibility.

Perhaps one could draw a parallel between this woman and "faithless Israel," the bride of the Lord God, who "has gone up on every high hill and under every spreading tree and has committed adultery there" [Jeremiah 3:6]. As a result of her acts of indecency, God says, "I gave faithless Israel her certificate of divorce and sent her away because of all her adulteries" [Jeremiah 3:8]. In speaking of His bride's attitude toward her unfaithfulness, God declared, "Because Israel's immorality mattered so little to her, she defiled the land and committed adultery with stone and wood" [Jeremiah 3:9].

By examining this parallel between Israel and the faithless wife of Deuteronomy 24, one can draw the reasonable conclusion that it was the latter's acts of immorality, and the attitude of complete indifference, and an unwillingness to change, that constituted her defilement. This view is given further validity when, in the Jeremiah text, the Lord alludes to Deuteronomy 24:1-4. Speaking of the immoralities of His bride, Israel, God states, "'If a man divorces his wife and she leaves him and marries another man, should he return to her again? Would not the land be completely defiled? But you have lived as a prostitute with many lovers—would you now return to Me?' declares the Lord" [Jeremiah 3:1].

A woman who has chosen a lifestyle of immorality, and is indifferent to all attempts to bring her to repentance, not only needs to be put away by her husband, since her unfaithfulness defiles the relationship, but she must never be taken back again, for the same reason. As was previously noted in Leviticus 21, it was not the state of divorce or widowhood that caused a woman to be considered defiled, and thus unsuitable for marriage to a priest of God, but rather prostitution. Those committed to righteousness and a spiritual relationship with their God, as well as the pursuit of the IDEAL in every area of life, simply must not bind themselves together with those of ungodly character [2 Corinthians 6:14-18].

In the Law of Moses God issued a challenge to His people to rise above the misery about them and strive for the IDEAL. To the degree they succeeded, their lives were blessed; to the degree they failed, they experienced distress. Those who refused to live up to God's call, and who inflicted suffering upon their spouses, God punished. For those who were victimized, God graciously and mercifully made provision in His Law for their relief.

A study of God's Law is, in many ways, a study of God's grace. In the face of man's failure, we see God's faithfulness; in the face of obstinacy and rejection, we behold patience and acceptance. After careful examination, we are led to acknowledge with David, "The law of the Lord is perfect, reviving the soul. The statutes of the Lord are trustworthy, making wise the simple. The precepts of the Lord are right, giving joy to the heart. The commands of the Lord are radiant, giving light to the eyes. The fear of the Lord is pure, enduring forever.

The ordinances of the Lord are sure and altogether righteous. They are more precious than gold, than much pure gold; they are sweeter than honey, than honey from the comb. By them is your servant warned; in keeping them there is great reward" [Psalm 19:7-11].

Radiating forth from out of God's Law are the warm, comforting rays of His marvelous love and justice, leading mankind ever upward toward His glorious IDEAL.

Chapter 2
The Historic & Poetic Books

Interspersed throughout the writings of the Old Testament, one beholds many marvelous examples of the tender affection with which God esteemed the people of Israel. They truly held a special place within His heart. Their cries of distress had moved Him to action, and in compassion He delivered them from out of a land of oppression and bondage. He brought them to Himself at Sinai, entered into a covenant with them, and established them as a holy nation; a kingdom of priests [Exodus 19]. He formed them into a powerful nation; protected them; provided for them; loved them.

Israel had been blessed above all other peoples upon the face of the earth. They were the chosen bride of deity; the delight of a loving and benevolent divine Husband. However, with unparalleled brazenness they repeatedly spurned His love for them, violating and defiling the covenant relationship which had been solemnly established in a spirit of trust. Israel, the faithless bride, sought out other lovers, committing acts of spiritual adultery with her pagan neighbors and their false deities. The bride of Almighty God had become a harlot!

With unimaginable patience, God sought to bring His bride to repentance and to restore the sanctity of His covenant relationship with her. Although there were brief periods of restoration, His efforts ultimately proved futile. The resolve of Israel was not to be swayed; her heart had been given to another. The time had finally come to officially terminate the relationship, although, in point of fact, Israel herself had effectively severed the union long before by her adulterous behavior. The issuance of the certificate of divorce was little more than a legal acknowledgment of the state of disunion; a disunion which, from a practical and realistic point of view, already existed.

In 722 B.C. the northern kingdom of Israel was carried away to a

43

foreign land by the Assyrians. God had issued His adulterous wife a certificate of divorce, and she had been led away to live with her pagan lovers. With His first marriage at an end, God turned to Judah, the sister of Israel, and formed a relationship with her. But Judah, like her sister, also became enthralled with the lure of the world, and was enticed into adulterous relationships.

"I gave faithless Israel her certificate of divorce and sent her away because of all her adulteries. Yet I saw that her unfaithful sister Judah had no fear; she also went out and committed adultery" [Jeremiah 3:8]. Although Judah did eventually return to her God, yet she "did not return to Me with all her heart, but only in pretense" [Jeremiah 3:10].

God finally reached a point in His relationship with Judah where He was forced to separate Himself from His unfaithful companion. This was not a divorce, as had been the case with Israel, but merely a separation. This separation took place in the form of the Babylonian Captivity, which lasted from 586 to 536 B.C. For the southern kingdom of Judah, this long separation from her Husband was not only a time of national humiliation and lamentation, but also an occasion which prompted some serious reflection. With increasing awareness of her sin and loss, came increasing transformation of both actions and attitudes. Judah began to view with renewed devotion the relationship she had had with her God, and which she was in danger of forfeiting permanently.

In the year 536 B.C. the long separation came to an end. Cyrus, founder and king of the great Persian empire, issued a declaration freeing the Jewish captives. Soon, a group of about 50,000 individuals, under the leadership of Zerubbabel, a prince in the house of David, set out on the 800 miles journey back to the holy city of Jerusalem. As might be expected, the people were anxious to return to their homeland, and to re-establish their long-neglected relationship with their God.

Twenty years later (516 B.C.), after numerous delays and discouragements, the new Temple was completed, thanks in large part to the efforts of such prophets as Haggai and Zechariah, who encouraged and strengthened the resolve of God's people during this difficult time. There were sounds of rejoicing heard throughout the city, spirits soared, and sacrifices were offered up to God in abundance [Ezra 6:15-22]. It seemed the relationship between God and His people was back on course.

Not a great deal of information is available concerning the next sixty years. Although the events of the book of Esther fall into this period of time, it primarily reflects life in the Persian capital rather than in the city of Jerusalem or its environs. We are aware, however, that intermarriage with pagan unbelievers was increasing at an alarming rate, as was the subsequent and inevitable adoption of their ungodly beliefs and practices. This racial and religious compromise was rapidly leading to an ever more visible deterioration in the spirituality of the Jewish people. Their relationship with God was again in jeopardy.

In the year 458 B.C., during the reign of the Persian king Artaxerxes I (also known as Longimanus, meaning "the long handed," because his right hand was reportedly larger than his left), Ezra secured permission to lead another group of Jews back to the holy city of Jerusalem. In the company of about 1500 of his countrymen, Ezra left the land of his people's captivity and set out for his beloved homeland [Ezra 7-8].

Upon his arrival, this descendant of Aaron, the first high priest of the people of Israel, found the situation to be far worse than he had imagined. The Jews were displaying a total disregard for the Law of Moses in virtually every area of their lives. They were also divorcing their lawful Jewish wives and entering into marriages with the pagan women of the area. Their compromise with the ungodly influences around them had so contaminated them that they faced the distinct possibility of extinction as a chosen, set-apart people. The situation was critical, and Ezra, who "was a teacher well-versed in the Law of Moses" [Ezra 7:6], soon determined that nothing less than a nation-wide reform of his people must be immediately initiated. Assisting him in this work of turning the people back to God was the prophet Malachi.

Ezra's first order of business on behalf of His God was to grapple with the complex problem of his countrymen's mixed marriages. The leaders in Jerusalem reported to Ezra the depth of this particular tragedy. "The people of Israel, including the priests and the Levites,

45

have not kept themselves separate from the neighboring peoples with their detestable practices, like those of the Canaanites, Hittites, Perizzites, Jebusites, Ammonites, Moabites, Egyptians and Amorites. They have taken some of their daughters as wives for themselves and their sons, and have mingled the holy race with the peoples around them. And the leaders and officials have led the way in this unfaithfulness" [Ezra 9:1-2].

After receiving this report, note the reaction of Ezra: "I tore my tunic and cloak, pulled hair from my head and beard and sat down appalled. Then everyone who trembled at the words of the God of Israel gathered around me because of this unfaithfulness of the exiles. And I sat there appalled until the evening sacrifice" [Ezra 9:3].

The Lord God has never looked favorably upon His people joining themselves intimately with the unrighteous peoples about them. Although they must of necessity dwell *in* the world, they nevertheless are frequently challenged from above never to become part *of* the world. In the prayer He uttered shortly before His arrest and subsequent crucifixion, Jesus did not ask that the Father remove His people from out of the world, but that He keep them away from the evil influences of the world about them [John 17].

The apostle Paul pointed out, in a quotation from Isaiah 52:11, that as a condition for maintaining a covenant relationship with God, His people must "come out from their midst (referring to the ungodly peoples of the world and their evil actions and attitudes) and be separate" [2 Corinthians 6:17]. "Do not be yoked together with unbelievers. For what do righteousness and wickedness have in common? Or what fellowship can light have with darkness? What harmony is there between Christ and Belial? What does a believer have in common with an unbeliever? What agreement is there between the temple of God and idols? For we are the temple of the living God. As God has said: 'I will live with them and walk among them, and I will be their God, and they will be My people'" [2 Corinthians 6:14-16].

The Jews of Ezra's time were violating all of these divine principles, and in so doing were in danger not only of losing their distinctiveness as a separate people, both racially and religiously, but also of losing their special relationship with their God. Furthermore, the Jewish men were dealing treacherously with the wives of their youth by casting them aside in favor of the foreign women of the land. Ezra was so appalled by the people's behavior that he sat in a state of shock until the time of the evening sacrifice.

"Then, at the evening sacrifice, I rose from my self-abasement, with my tunic and cloak torn, and fell on my knees with my hands spread out to the Lord my God and prayed" [Ezra 9:5-6a]. Ezra's heartfelt prayer, which is recorded in vs. 6b-15, is without a doubt one of the most moving appeals unto God, and confession of a people's guilt and shame, found anywhere in the Bible. It obviously touched others among God's people as well, for "while Ezra was praying and confessing, weeping and throwing himself down before the house of God, a large crowd of Israelites—men, women and children—gathered around him. They too wept bitterly" [Ezra 10:1].

By intermarrying with foreign women, the people of God had broken a direct command of the Law. Moses charged the Israelites with these words: "Do not intermarry with them. Do not give your daughters to their sons or take their daughters for your sons, for they will turn your sons away from following Me to serve other gods, and the Lord's anger will burn against you and will quickly destroy you" [Deuteronomy 7:3-6]. This was exactly what was happening among the returned captives, and as a result they were in grave danger of experiencing the consuming wrath of the Lord. Decisive action had to be taken if this impending destruction was to be avoided, and it had to be enacted quickly.

The only action that would suffice in this tragic and painful situation was the complete severing of all intimate, interpersonal relationships with these pagan peoples; relationships which had been entered into in direct violation of God's Law. The suggestion that this course of action was the one which should be taken was made by a man named Shecaniah, who said, "We have been unfaithful to our God by marrying foreign women from the peoples around us. But in spite of this, there is still hope for Israel. Now let us make a covenant before our God to send away all these women and their children, in accordance with the

47

counsel of my lord and of those who fear the commands of our God. Let it be done according to the Law" [Ezra 10:2-3].

A proclamation was sent forth throughout the land instructing all the people of Judah to assemble themselves in Jerusalem within three days time. Those who failed to appear would forfeit all their possessions, and would additionally be expelled from the assembly of God's people.

On the twentieth day of the ninth month, the people gathered themselves together before the house of God. They sat huddled together in the midst of a driving rain storm, trembling because of the inclement weather and the distressing nature of that which had brought them together on this fearful occasion. Ezra stood before the throng and addressed them with words which pierced to the depths of their hearts: "You have been unfaithful; you have married foreign women, adding to Israel's guilt. Now make confession to the Lord, the God of your fathers, and do His will. Separate yourselves from the peoples around you and from your foreign wives" [Ezra 10:10-11].

Although there were a few who were simply unwilling to go along with this advice [vs. 15], most realized they had disobeyed the commands of their God and needed to restore their relationship with Him. Thus, "they all gave their hands in pledge to put away their wives, and for their guilt they each presented a ram from the flock as a guilt offering" [vs. 19]. This tragedy was compounded by the fact that "some of them had children by these wives" [vs. 44].

Nehemiah, the royal cup-bearer to King Artaxerxes I, returned to Jerusalem from the land of captivity about this time to assist Ezra and Malachi in this much needed spiritual reformation. The rebuke of Ezra was mild in comparison to the indignation felt by the righteous Nehemiah as he witnessed the transgressions of his people. "I rebuked them and called curses down on them. I beat some of the men and pulled out their hair" [Nehemiah 13:25]. He challenged them to reflect upon their own history so as to perceive the folly of their behavior. "Was it not because of marriages like these that Solomon king of Israel sinned? Among the many nations there was no king like him. He was loved by his God, and God made him king over all Israel, but even he

DOWN, BUT NOT OUT

was led into sin by foreign women. Must we hear now that you too are doing all this terrible wickedness and are being unfaithful to our God by marrying foreign women?" [vs. 26-27].

The passages which one must carefully note in this rather lengthy historical account are the following: "Now let us make a covenant before our God to send away all these women and their children ... let it be done according to the Law" [Ezra 10:3]. "Do His will. Separate yourselves from ... your foreign wives" [Ezra 10:11]. "We have been unfaithful to our God by marrying foreign women from the peoples around us. But in spite of this, there is still hope for Israel" [Ezra 10:2].

God's people were in violation of His Law. They were guilty of being unfaithful to their Lord, and to the covenant they had entered into with Him. But, they were not without hope! Their relationship with Him could still be restored if they would turn away from their pagan wives and turn back to Him. It is clearly stated that the putting away of these women would be an act of compliance with His will.

As might be expected, not a few are greatly troubled by these passages, and indeed by this whole series of events involving God's people and their pagan spouses. Is it not somewhat inconsistent, they reason, for God to declare, "I hate divorce," and then insist upon it, or at least seemingly condone it, on such a massive scale?! Attempts have been made to "cast God in a more favorable light" by theorizing that these Jewish men were not actually married to the foreign women; that they were just "living in sin" with them. This, however, fails to seriously consider the clear statements within the text to the contrary. The relationships in question are referred to as marriages, not as continuing acts of fornication or adultery. The women are termed "wives," not mistresses, concubines, or harlots. The fact that these men are told to put away these wives, by whom many of them had fathered children, also implies far more of a relationship than would be evident in a casual affair.

One simply cannot gloss over the fact that these were marriages. The problem was, they were relationships entered into in direct violation of the will of God as revealed through the Law of Moses. The Lord had specifically informed His people, "Thou shalt not marry foreign women," and yet they had chosen to do so anyway.

The inevitable consequences of their sinful rebellion were many. The intermingling of the Jews with the peoples of the neighboring nations would eventually result in a people who were a mixture of numerous different races, religions and cultures. No longer would they be a unique, set apart people as God intended; no longer would their lineage be pure. Paganism, and its accompanying idolatry and immorality, would begin to infest the worship of the one true God. The Lord would ultimately be cast aside in favor of the false deities. As Nehemiah pointed out, this had happened to Solomon, and it was about to happen again.

It was absolutely critical the Jews maintain their purity, both as a people and as a religion. This purity and distinctiveness were being endangered by their violation of God's Law with respect to intermarrying with foreign women. In order to set the nation back on the right course, radical measures were called for. In this particular case, the only solution was to remove the cause of the impurity, which was the pagan wives.

The covenant relationship of the Lord God with His people, which had been established prior to the unlawful unions of the Jews with their foreign wives, and the national distinctiveness of the Jewish people, was far more vital to God's eternal plan than the relationships of a few men with some of the local women. God's eternal plan to send the Messiah into the world for the redemption of mankind through a specific lineage was in great jeopardy by virtue of this rush to non-Jewish relationships. So much was at stake for the spiritual future of mankind, that these unlawful marriages simply could not be allowed to exist. For the benefit of humanity throughout all future generations, both Jew and Gentile, they had to be terminated. For the ultimate good of the many, the few must suffer.

Were people going to experience hurt and pain as a result of this process? Yes. Anytime men willfully transgress God's will and IDEAL for their lives, people suffer. It is an inevitable consequence of sin. It is also a sad fact of our human existence that when individuals sin, innocent people often are harmed as well. One cannot help but experience deep feelings for the children of these unlawful unions, for example. But, at the same time, one must not overlook the central truth that all of this pain and tragedy was brought on by a refusal to obey God. Had His commands simply been obeyed, this entire agonizing situation could have been avoided. The blame for the suffering they were undergoing could be cast nowhere else than at their own feet.

God's eternal purposes for mankind would go forward; nothing would be allowed to stand in the way of the fulfillment of His will. God hates divorce, and He hates what happens to people when divorce occurs. Without question, God hated what had to be done in this unique situation in order that His eternal, redemptive plan could be enacted for the good of mankind. Relationships were going to be terminated, and that meant a lot of pain and distress, and undoubtedly this greatly grieved God. Nevertheless, this situation had deteriorated to the point where His plan for the ultimate salvation of mankind through the coming Messiah, who would descend through Judah, could well have been seriously jeopardized. The time for action had come, traumatic though it would prove to be.

At times, through their sinful, rebellious actions, men place themselves and others in situations and circumstances where there is simply no painless means of extrication. One has journeyed so far down the wrong pathway that no matter what course one adopts in an effort to return to the right path, others are going to be harmed. In such cases one is essentially faced with only two logical choices: continue on the wrong path or turn back to God.

In the case of the Jewish men of Ezra's time, the plan they chose to adopt was the only one which would ultimately place them back on the right path, both individually and as a nation. It was a difficult and painful decision; a decision which caused tremendous grief to many innocent people; a decision which even pained God, for He takes no delight in the sufferings of mankind. Excruciating though it was, there was no other recourse.

There are those in the religious world who detect in this sorrowful account an indication of God's approval of the state of divorce. They infer that if God commanded it of His people in this particular situation that He must thereby find it acceptable in all situations. What God *allows* and what God *approves*, however, are often vastly dissimilar. Jesus pointed out that God permitted divorce, but it was far from pleasing in His eyes. It was God's will that the pagan wives be put away, but His feelings about the matter are reflected in the words of Malachi 2:16, "'I hate divorce,' says the Lord God of Israel." Remember, this statement is made in the writings of the prophet who assisted Ezra and Nehemiah in bringing about the needed reforms in Judah, a major part of which was the severing of the unions with the pagan wives.

No, God does *not* approve of divorce. It fails to achieve His IDEAL, regardless of the extenuating circumstances. One should exercise extreme caution in such interpretive matters lest God be characterized as condoning, either directly or indirectly, the pain and suffering which men frequently inflict upon themselves by their sinful behavior. When men choose to reject His IDEAL, the responsibility for the consequences subsequently suffered are man's alone. To view this account as a source of biblical justification for the termination of a covenant relationship with one's spouse is to completely misunderstand the purpose of the text. This dark page in the history of God's people has been preserved through the ages not for the purpose of justifying divorce, but to motivate mankind to increased efforts to achieve the IDEAL, in light of the horrors that await them should they fail to do so!

One thing which must absolutely be stressed at this point is that in spite of the somewhat negative nature of this narrative, God's people were still very much in possession of HOPE! In the words of Shecaniah to Ezra, "In spite of this, there is still hope for Israel!" [Ezra 10:2]. In counseling with those undergoing the trauma of marital distress and disunion, one will often hear them say, with despair in their voices, "I just don't feel like there's any hope for me." A shattered marriage is a terrible blow to the entire system: physically, emotionally and spiritually. Physical illnesses often increase, emotional distress seems more frequent and acute, and spiritually one often feels cast off by both God and His people. For far too many this knockdown blow soon becomes a knockout blow.

A woman once remarked, "God could never love me or accept me. I'm divorced!" Another young woman described, between sobs of despair, how the wife of one of her church's leaders informed her that because she was divorced and remarried she was doomed to hell, but that she should bring her children to church so that at least *they* could have some hope of salvation. While proclaiming the Word of God in Germany some years ago, this author was approached by a family desirous of worshipping and serving with our local assembly of believers. Their concern was that they would not be accepted into our midst, since they had been barred entrance to the building at their previous location for having committed "an unpardonable sin."

"You blasphemed the Holy Spirit?" "No," she replied dejectedly, "even worse. My husband divorced me and I remarried."

Such examples could be multiplied almost endlessly. The world is filled with hurting people, and, oftentimes, the very ones who should be promoting the healing and the lifting up of the fallen, are instead guilty of inflicting even further pain upon them. If the Lord God, in His infinite grace and mercy, is willing to extend forgiveness, acceptance and hope to those who have stumbled and fallen, His people dare not do any less! The physically, emotionally, and spiritually battered and bruised must be welcomed into our midst with open arms, and the healing salve of the Lord's love applied to their wounds. As ambassadors of God's wondrous grace, our message to the downtrodden must ever be the truth immortalized in the words of Shecaniah: "In spite of this, there is still hope!"

As our examination of the Old Covenant scriptures continues, we discover that the only other specific reference found within the inspired historical writings with regard to the breakdown of a marital relationship and a subsequent remarriage is contained in the book of Esther. This ancient account describes events which occurred shortly *before* the situation just discussed in Ezra and Nehemiah.

In the year 486 B.C., Darius I, monarch of the vast Persian empire, was slain while attempting to quell an Egyptian revolt. Although an extremely cruel man toward his enemies, he nevertheless proved to be quite benevolent toward the people of Israel. Darius used his great power as king to assist in quieting the opposition of some malicious malcontents to the rebuilding of the Temple. He even went so far as to issue funds to the Jews from out of the royal treasury to expedite their work of constructing a house of worship for their God. The text of this royal decree is preserved for us within the pages of the Scriptures [Ezra 6:6-12].

Upon the death of Darius I, his son, Xerxes I (also known as Ahasuerus), ascended to the throne of the Persian empire. Xerxes had the distinction of being the grandson of Cyrus (the monarch who ended the Babylonian captivity of the Jews), since his father had married Atossa, the daughter of Cyrus. Xerxes was 35 years old when he took the throne in 486 B.C.

Upon assuming power, this young ruler quickly brought the Egyptian revolt, which had cost his father his life, under complete control. During the twenty years of his reign he was able to effectively repel several other revolts against Persian domination. His only significant failure in this regard was in putting down the Greek rebellion. Unlike other nations around them, who were in unwilling but quiet submission to Persian power, the Greeks were able to win their freedom, and over a century later, under the leadership of Alexander the Great, they would rise up and put an end to the once mighty Persian empire.

Religiously, Xerxes was a Zoroastrian. This religion was based on the teachings of Zoroaster, who, according to Persian tradition, was born around 660 B.C. With regard to his personality, Xerxes was reputed to have behaved habitually as a spoiled child. He was extremely susceptible to flattery, and he loved surrounding himself with the pomp and trappings of royalty.

His reign came to a sudden end when he was assassinated by Artabanus, the captain of his bodyguard. Artabanus reigned for about seven months, at which time he himself was assassinated by Artaxerxes, the third son of the slain Xerxes. It was this son, after becoming king, who granted Ezra and Nehemiah permission to return with two groups of Jews to enact the previously discussed reforms in Jerusalem.

The primary significance of Xerxes I, however, with regard to the

Jewish people and the focus of this particular study, is that he was the Persian monarch who married Esther, whose story is preserved in the biblical book bearing the same name.

According to the account, in the third year of his reign Xerxes decided to host a week long banquet for all his nobles and officials. "Wine was served in goblets of gold, each one different from the other, and the royal wine was abundant, in keeping with the king's liberality. By the king's command each guest was allowed to drink in his own way, for the king instructed all the wine stewards to serve each man what he wished" [Esther 1:7-8]. Apparently, this was little more than a week long opportunity to indulge the various desires of the flesh in the king's presence and with the king's approval.

On the seventh day of the festivities, while "King Xerxes was in high spirits from the wine" [vs. 10], he commanded his eunuchs to bring his wife, Queen Vashti, to the banquet hall so that she could "display her beauty to the people and nobles, for she was lovely to look at" [vs. 11]. It is believed by some scholars that what the king was here demanding of Vashti was that she dance before the people, exposing herself in the process, so that his nobles and officials could admire her body, and thus envy him for possessing such an exquisite wife. Queen Vashti, however, in an unheard of act of defiance, refused to comply with his wishes, and chose not even to come near the banquet area. "Then the king became furious and burned with anger" [vs. 12].

The king's chief advisors conveyed to him their concern over this most serious matter. Vashti was setting a precedent in the land that could well prove to be very discomforting for the men. In effect, they accused her of initiating a "women's rights movement," an "evil" which simply could not be allowed to exist within the empire. An advisor by the name of Memucan summed up the situation and proposed a solution that probably best reflected the thinking of most of the men close to the king: "Queen Vashti has done wrong, not only against the king but also against all the nobles and the peoples of all the provinces of King Xerxes. For the queen's conduct will become known to all the women, and so they will despise their husbands and say, 'King Xerxes commanded Queen Vashti to be brought before him, but she would not come.' This very day the Persian and Median women of the nobility who have heard about the queen's conduct will respond to all the king's nobles in the same way. There will be no end of disrespect and discord. Therefore, if it pleases the king, let him issue a royal decree and let it be written in the laws of Persia and Media, which cannot be repealed, that Vashti is never again to enter the presence of King Xerxes. Also let the king give her royal position to someone else who is better than she. Then when the king's edict is proclaimed throughout all his vast realm, all the women will respect their husbands, from the least to the greatest" [vs. 16-20].

This advice pleased the king, and, understandably, it pleased the nobles and officials as well. By royal decree women would be kept in their place, and the queen would pay a dear price for stepping out of it! Therefore, Xerxes sent a proclamation to every corner of his kingdom declaring it to be a law of the realm "that every man should be ruler over his own household" [vs. 22].

Were these events not so tragic, one might almost find them humorous. The thought of these powerful men huddled together trying to devise a legal means of acquiring and maintaining respect from their wives is ludicrous. However, they accomplished at least one good thing: they provided the world with a timeless reminder of an ageless truth — He who must demand respect, is not worthy of it!

The action the king was advised to take against his queen essentially amounted to a divorce. Their relationship was to be publicly and officially terminated, which, it was hoped, would serve as an example to other wives who might be tempted to show disrespect toward their husbands. No longer was Vashti to enjoy any of the privileges associated with being the wife of the king. She was forbidden from even entering his presence ever again, and her position as queen was to be given to another woman. This was about as complete a destruction of the relationship as one could accomplish, short of death.

What became of Vashti after this point in history is unknown. She is never mentioned again. Whatever her ultimate fate, this wonderful, courageous woman, who prized her moral integrity above her crown, and who dared to stand up boldly to a self-centered pagan monarch and insist upon a woman's right to be shown dignity and respect, will forever live as one of the genuine heroines of history!!

When King Xerxes finally started to sober up, and his anger subsided, he began to realize the full extent of his ill-advised over-reaction. Realizing that their king was growing agitated over his decision, his attendants suggested that a search of the entire realm be made for "beautiful young virgins for the king" [Esther 2:2]. If one could be located who pleased him, she should be crowned queen in Vashti's place.

This idea pleased Xerxes, so the plan was put into action. The long, intense process of searching the realm for the right young maiden ended with the selection of a young Jewish girl (although she did not at first reveal her racial heritage) by the name of Hadassah. Later, perhaps at her coronation, she would be given a Persian name, Esther (meaning "star"), by which she is better known.

Esther grew up as an orphan, being raised by her cousin Mordecai, who "had taken her as his own daughter when her father and mother died" [Esther 2:7]. "Now the young lady was beautiful of form and face" [vs. 7], and "Esther won the favor of everyone who saw her" [vs. 15]. Even though King Xerxes had a large number of beautiful young virgins from which to choose (the ancient Jewish historian Josephus put the number at 400), "the king was attracted to Esther more than to any of the other women, and she won his favor and approval more than any of the other virgins. So he set a royal crown on her head and made her queen instead of Vashti. The king gave a great banquet for all his nobles and officials in honor of Esther. He proclaimed a holiday throughout the provinces and distributed gifts with royal liberality" [vs. 17-18].

In the account before us, we are faced not only with an apparent divorce, but also a remarriage. Some have found it rather difficult to understand how Mordecai and Esther could have been willing participants in this series of events, especially in light of the later attitudes and actions of Ezra and Nehemiah toward the mixed marriages that were occurring back in Jerusalem. Although it is true that the actual reforms of these two men were still several years in the future, the sentiment that this practice was wrong should nevertheless have been very much in evidence among the Jewish exiles, of whom Mordecai and Esther were a part.

Is it possible they were unaware that God, in His Law, had specifically forbidden intermarrying with foreigners? Questions such as this simply are not addressed within the pages of the book of Esther. Indeed, this document never once even mentions the Divine Name. Having spent their entire lives in a pagan land, one can only speculate as to the extent of their knowledge concerning God's Law and His specific expectations for their lives. This certainly in no way is meant to excuse their actions, but perhaps it does assist one in understanding them.

It should also not be overlooked that Mordecai and Esther may well have been given little choice in the matter. In the Hebrew text of this account, Esther was said to have been "taken" to the king's palace and placed into the "custody" of Hegai, the eunuch in charge of the king's women. The word "taken" is the Hebrew verb "laqah" which can convey the concept "taken by force." If this was what occurred, the situation may have been far more coercive than consensual.

Five years pass. During this period of time Mordecai and Haman, one of the king's chief officers, become bitter enemies. Mordecai had refused to bow before Haman and display what the latter deemed to be proper respect. Rather than inflict punishment only upon Mordecai, Haman decided to inflict it upon the entire Jewish population. He convinced Xerxes to issue a decree commanding that the Jews be completely exterminated from the land. "Dispatches were sent by couriers to all the king's provinces with the order to destroy, kill and annihilate all the Jews — young and old, women and little children — on a single day, the thirteenth day of the twelfth month, the month of Adar, and to plunder their goods" [Esther 3:13-14].

When Mordecai learned of this diabolical plan he sent a message to Esther, appealing with her to convince the king to withdraw this genocidal decree. To make a lengthy account more brief, Esther eventually determined that her only recourse was to reveal to Xerxes that she too was a Jew, and thus one of the very people he had ordered annihilated. She further informed the king of Haman's conspiracy, and that it was prompted by his hatred of her cousin Mordecai.

When Xerxes realized he had been manipulated, he was furious. To help rectify the injustice done to Mordecai, the king had him promoted, and ordered Haman hanged upon the very gallows he had had constructed for the purpose of executing Mordecai. To his consternation, however, Xerxes knew that it was impossible for him to rescind an official order that had already been sent throughout the empire. Thus, Xerxes did the next best thing: he issued a decree allowing the Jewish people to defend themselves against those who sought to carry out his original command to exterminate them.

The Jews fought valiantly, and many thousands who came against them were slain. When the battles were over, and the people of God had prevailed, they assembled together for a great victory feast, which is known as *Purim*, a feast still celebrated to this day among the Jewish people.

Through the intercession of Queen Esther, one of their own, the Jews were spared a devastating slaughter. A statement made by Mordecai to Esther may well shed some light on how God viewed this entire situation of Esther's marriage to Xerxes. "Who knows but that you have come to royal position for such a time as this?" [Esther 4:14]. The obvious implication of this statement is that the Lord God may well have providentially placed Esther in a relationship with this king for the very purpose of providing a deliverer for those of His people still living in exile during this most critical time. Indeed, not a few scholars view this entire account as a classic illustration of God's *providence*; a divine interaction within the course of human events clearly suggested by Mordecai's statement to Esther.

Some have deduced from the above apparent interaction of God with the historical events of that time a tacit approval, at least in this one case, of intermarriage with a foreigner, and of a relationship with one who has put away a spouse for no just cause. If God were to approve it in *this* case, would He not perhaps also approve of *other* such cases? Thus, a few detect here an open door to a more liberal appraisal of divorce and remarriage.

The assumption of divine approval, however, may well be going far beyond the actual intent of the text, or of the historical circumstances which it depicts. A more logical interpretation, and one certainly more consistent with the remainder of God's revelation, is the concept that the Lord is capable of utilizing even a negative circumstance to effect a positive result. Such a view detracts neither from the providence of God, nor His direct interaction with the events of human history.

It is difficult to conceive of God being in any way pleased with Xerxes' dismissal of Vashti. Nor can one easily conceive of Him taking any pleasure in a young Jewish maiden being "taken" and placed, perhaps forcibly, into a relationship with such a godless pagan monarch. But, it is not difficult at all to conceive of our God utilizing such events, as they transpire in history, to accomplish His purposes and to further His plan for humanity. Had Esther not been in the favorable position she was in, from the standpoint of her influence upon the king, God would simply have utilized another method for delivering His people from the slaughter proposed by Haman. Even Mordecai himself realized this great truth. Just before telling Esther that she may well have been in her present position for the purpose of effecting her people's salvation, he observed, "If you remain silent at this time, relief and deliverance for the Jews will arise from another place" [Esther 4:14].

The will of God will always be accomplished! He can either work through us, around us, or in spite of us, but His purposes shall always be achieved. Although Esther's circumstances in life were far from the IDEAL, through no fault of her own, she was nevertheless in the right place at the right time to be used by God to effect a grand deliverance for His people.

Must one assume, because of the negative circumstances of life that were thrust upon her, that Esther stood condemned before her God? Was she to be eternally cast off by the Lord because of her union with a divorced pagan monarch? The text itself affirms no such rejection or condemnation. Such a conclusion would have to be drawn without the support of the Scriptures. Indeed, if God could bring about a great victory for Israel through the efforts of a prostitute from Jericho named

Rahab, even singling her out twice in the pages of the New Testament documents as an example of faith [Hebrews 11:31; James 2:25], why could He not also show equal love, mercy and acceptance toward the young maiden Esther? Would the God of grace, in fact, do any less?

Also listed in the Scriptures as one of God's faithful servants was a man named Samson [Hebrews 11:32], who took a Philistine woman as a wife. Was this not in direct violation of the Law of Moses? His father and mother asked him, "Isn't there an acceptable woman among your relatives or among all our people? Must you go to the uncircumcised Philistines to get a wife?" However, Samson replied, "Get her for me. She's the right one for me." The passage then explains the purpose of this seemingly ungodly and rebellious union: "His parents did not know that this was from the Lord, who was seeking an occasion to confront the Philistines; for at that time they were ruling over Israel" [Judges 14:1-4]. Once again, the providence of God is seen at work, and in what some might characterize a most unorthodox manner. Nevertheless, His will for His people was being accomplished, and by a methodology which He Himself had chosen.

Difficult though it may be for those with a strictly legalistic religious perspective to accept, there have been occasions when, to accomplish specific purposes, God has allowed, and even encouraged, the violation of His Law, with no resulting guilt on the part of the violators. A perfect example is found in Matthew 12:1-8 in which Jesus speaks of an event in the life of David and some of his associates. Because they were extremely hungry, they "entered the house of God, and he and his companions ate the consecrated bread — which was not lawful for them to do, but only for the priests." Was David condemned by the Son of God for this blatant violation of the Law of Moses? Did God punish David for transgressing His Law? Just the opposite! Jesus declared David free of guilt, and He then proceeded to rebuke the religionists and legalists of His day for "condemning the innocent."

As Jesus clearly demonstrates, the Lord God is far more concerned with acts of compassion, than acts of sacrifice; with spirituality, than legalism; with internals, than externals; with relationship, than religion. This is certainly not to discredit or negate the importance of God's

Law. It served a vital purpose. The Law directed men toward the IDEAL; it focused their minds upon those actions and attitudes which fell short of that IDEAL, so that they might be avoided; it even, at times, validated the infliction of punishment for those failures so that they might not be repeated. The Law in many ways was a tutor leading men upward toward the attainment of an ultimate goal, an IDEAL. The Law itself was never meant to be viewed as an end in itself, or as indispensable. It was a tool; a means to an end. It served man, not vice versa. Thus, exceptions to Law were not unknown; on occasion, should the situation merit it, the Law could be set aside, and without guilt or consequence. Perhaps Jesus summed it up best when He declared, during the above discussion, "The Sabbath was made for man, and not man for the Sabbath" [Mark 2:27].

The religionists of Jesus' day were appalled at His unprecedented display of compassion and acceptance toward those whose lives fell short of the IDEAL. Yes, He *could* have spoken words of condemnation against these many sinners. They were indeed violators of Law, and He certainly had the legal right to pronounce condemnation. Instead, in a spirit of love and mercy, Jesus forgave them and challenged them to begin striving anew to achieve God's IDEAL. By focusing entirely on law, men had lost sight of such qualities as grace, mercy, compassion, love, forgiveness, and acceptance. Determined to bind and enforce the letter of the law at any cost, in a misguided and misinformed zeal for their God and their traditions, they often inflicted tremendous harm upon one another.

There were many times when Jesus did in fact condemn those about Him who were living godless lives, but a careful reading of the Scriptures will display that these were largely those so steeped in their religious traditions and their love of law that they had failed to exhibit the love, mercy and compassion that God actually desired. To the Rahabs, Samsons and Esthers of this world, the Lord has always shown tremendous care and concern. The challenge before mankind is to go and do likewise!

Turning one's attention to the poetic writings of the Old Testament, it becomes quickly apparent that the failure of men and women to attain and maintain God's IDEAL, with respect to marital relationships, is simply not a major focus of these writings. About the closest one can come to such teachings are some of the sentiments expressed in selected proverbs.

Note the following examples: "Better to live on a corner of the roof than share a house with a quarrelsome wife" [Proverbs 21:9; 25:24]. "Better to live in a desert than with a quarrelsome and ill-tempered wife" [Proverbs 21:19]. Although it is true that these passages don't deal directly with divorce, nevertheless they do reflect a commonly held sentiment: separation was preferable to a contentious, tumultuous relationship.

Whether or not these sentiments expressed proverbially within the pages of Scripture in any way reflect God's sentiments, or indicate His approval of separation for such causes, has long been the subject of heated debate. Some feel Paul may well have had these passages partially in mind when writing the following advice to the church in Corinth: "But if the unbeliever leaves, let him do so. A believing man or woman is not bound in such circumstances; God has called us to live in *peace*" [1 Corinthians 7:15].

Regardless of the interpretation one places upon the passages from Proverbs, few will disagree with the assessment that any breakdown of a marital relationship, regardless of the cause, is a tragedy and falls short of God's IDEAL. Ideally, nothing will separate the parties to a covenant of marriage. However, when spouses begin losing sight of one another, and engaging in selfish contentions and struggles, damage to a relationship is not far behind. If anything, these passages are an endorsement of the IDEAL, in that they display the heartache and loss of peace which occurs when couples fail to strive for the IDEAL, and instead strive with one another.

In Proverbs 2:16-17 one discovers "the adulteress ... the wayward wife ... who has left the partner of her youth and ignored the covenant she made before God." Solomon advises his son that one who is wise will avoid such behavior, and will also avoid those engaged in it. To choose otherwise, as the text goes on to explain, leads to destruction.

In a far more positive light, there are many truly marvelous and moving depictions of the IDEAL contained within the poetic books of the Old Testament. One cannot help but call to mind the poetic professions of love and admiration and mutual delight expressed in the Song of Solomon. A more moving tribute to a couple's love one would be hard-pressed to find.

Any study of successful marriage would be incomplete without time spent examining the words penned by King Lemuel in Proverbs 31:10-31. This depiction of the worthy woman, as taught to him by his mother, is unequaled in literature.

Before continuing with this study, the reader is encouraged to take the time to carefully read both the Song of Solomon and the above passage from Proverbs 31. Allowing oneself to be caught up in the beauty of God's IDEAL for marriage will prove not only personally refreshing at this point, but will also help one to better appreciate the depth of loss experienced when these sacred covenant relationships break down.

Chapter 3
The Prophetic Books

Within the canon of the Old Testament writings there are sixteen books classified as prophetic. These are generally subdivided into two additional groups: The Major Prophets (4 books) and the Minor Prophets (12 books). Among the four prophets of the former grouping, only Isaiah and Jeremiah discuss the topic of divorce and remarriage; of the latter grouping of prophets, only Hosea, Micah, and Malachi speak specifically to this subject.

THE PROPHET ISAIAH

The time during which Isaiah actively served His God spanned from the reign of King Uzziah, the 10th king of the southern kingdom of Judah, to the reign of King Hezekiah, the 13th king of Judah. This would place the bulk of his prophetic ministry during the latter half of the eighth century B.C. This was a time in history which witnessed the increasing decline of the northern kingdom of Israel, and its ultimate fall in 722 B.C. to the Assyrians. The southern kingdom of Judah also seemed ready to follow in the footsteps of her sister Israel. However, partially through the tireless efforts of this great prophet of God, disaster was temporarily averted. It would be another 136 years before Judah was led away into the Babylonian captivity.

Isaiah's ministry was directed primarily toward the people of Jerusalem and its environs. According to Jewish tradition, he was the cousin of King Uzziah, which may well explain what some scholars feel to be an unusually easy and open access to the kings of his nation, and his apparent intimacy with the priesthood. From the wording of Isaiah 8:3 ("Then I went to the prophetess, and she conceived and gave birth to a son"), there seems to be little doubt that Isaiah's wife also served

God in the prophetic ministry.

Throughout his public service to God and His people, Isaiah called his fellow countrymen to lives of renewed holiness and devotion unto the Lord. The descendants of Israel were a covenant people, and they needed both to realize that fact and to begin behaving as such. His message was not always popular nor well received among this rebellious people, but it was one that, for their own spiritual and national well-being, had to be proclaimed.

According to the Jewish *Mishna*, Isaiah was martyred during the reign of King Manasseh, the 14th king of Judah. From the testimony of several other ancient sources, he died by being sawn in half with a wooden saw [*The Ascension of Isaiah*, 2nd century A.D.; Justin Martyr's *Dialogue with Trypho*, c. 150 A.D.; and Epiphanius' work *Lives of the Prophets*, 4th century A.D.]. Some scholars see a possible allusion to Isaiah's martyrdom in the book of Hebrews: "They were stoned; they were sawed in two; they were put to death by the sword" [Hebrews 11:37].

In the writings of the prophet Isaiah, with reference to the focus of this study, the Lord said, "Where is your mother's certificate of divorce with which I sent her away?" [Isaiah 50:1]. At this point in time, God had not yet given His unfaithful spouse over to her pagan lovers; the covenant of marriage was still in force. Still willing to take her back, if she would repent of her adulteries, God had refrained from issuing the certificate of divorce. Thus, the purpose of asking for the whereabouts of this document was for the purpose of demonstrating to the people that it did not exist. His patience had not yet run out; there was still hope for reconciliation.

The above question also clearly implies which party to the covenant must bear the responsibility for the breakdown of the relationship. God did not cast off His spouse, nor had He officially terminated their marriage — "Where is the document that would prove such a charge?," He asks. It was Israel who chose to be unfaithful to the covenant, and to pursue other lovers, and to risk the destruction of the relationship.

Nevertheless, God hoped for a reconciliation with His unfaithful spouse. In Isaiah 54:4-8 the Lord clearly states His willingness to forgive and forget; and, contingent upon her willingness to repent and return to Him, His willingness to continue in a loving, accepting covenant with His bride. He assured her that she would not be made to suffer shame, nor would she be disgraced by her former actions. "With deep compassion I will bring you back" [vs. 7]. God admits to His spouse, "in a surge of anger I hid my face from you for a moment" [vs. 8], an understandable emotion in light of her adulteries. However, He was now willing to show compassion to her, even though she had shown none toward Him. Because of His surpassing love for Israel, God was calling her back [vs. 6], "For your Maker is your husband — the Lord Almighty is His name — the Holy One of Israel is your Redeemer; He is called the God of all the earth" [vs. 5].

There is no question but what God had every "legal right" to end this relationship because of the repeated adulteries of His faithless spouse. Had God been seeking reasons to sever His covenant with Israel, they were supplied by the latter in abundance. However, God's covenant with Israel was perceived as being so precious that He was willing to forego His "legal rights" in order to pursue every possible avenue for preserving this relationship. In the sight of God, His spouse, and His covenant with her, were far more important than any "rights" He might justifiably have hastened to exercise. God's hope was for reconciliation, regardless of the hurt that had been inflicted upon Him; a hope not surrendered easily.

It was only Israel's complete and utter rejection of Him, and an absolute refusal to repent and return, that caused Him finally, and with deep sorrow, to "officially" terminate the covenant of marriage by means of a certificate of divorce. This was more a formality than anything else, as the covenant had already been broken, and the relationship had long since ended, as a result of the unfaithfulness of Israel. That God waited as long as He did before recognizing "officially" the reality of His situation, demonstrates His loving patience, willingness to forgive, and desire for reconciliation.

History clearly reveals that Israel repeatedly refused the gracious offers of her Husband. Time and again she spurned His loving advances. Finally, the Lord God was left with no alternative but to acknowledge the inevitable: the marriage was at an end. The pleas issued through Isaiah were rejected; it was left to Jeremiah to record the divorce.

THE PROPHET JEREMIAH

In the year 626 B.C., in the 13th year of the reign of King Josiah, Judah's 16th king, a young man by the name of Jeremiah began his prophetic ministry to the people of the southern kingdom. Probably only 18 to 20 years old at the time of his calling, he would faithfully serve His God for the next 50 years of his life. He came from the Levitical town of Anathoth in the territory of Benjamin, and was from a family of priests.

As a prophet of God, Jeremiah was noted for several qualities: A tremendous love for his people, and a willingness to demonstrate it; a zeal for God, and a willingness to speak out for Him even when it was not popular to do so. Perhaps his best known characteristics, though, were his tender heart and compassionate spirit. It was not uncommon to behold Jeremiah weeping publicly over the sins and rebellion of his people as they turned farther away from their Lord. At one point he exclaimed, "Oh, that my head were a spring of water and my eyes a fountain of tears! I would weep day and night for the slain of my people" [Jeremiah 9:1].

Contributing to his sense of grief was the fact that this sensitive prophet witnessed one evil king after another ascend to the throne of his beloved Judah; he watched as anarchy spread through the land like a malignant growth; and, in spite of his repeated efforts, he beheld his countrymen increasingly reject the loving advances of their God. He additionally had the misfortune of witnessing, and indeed experiencing, the downfall of his homeland in 586 B.C. and the subsequent Babylonian captivity.

Further, he was mocked, slandered, afflicted and persecuted by the very people he was seeking to bring to repentance. "I am ridiculed all day long; everyone mocks me. Whenever I speak, I cry out proclaiming violence and destruction. So the word of the Lord has brought me insult and reproach all day long" [Jeremiah 20:7-8]. On one occasion he became so discouraged he cursed the day he was born, determined he would never speak another word for God to this obstinate people [Jeremiah 20]. On yet another occasion he was ready to throw in the towel, get as far away from the people of God as he could, and open a "lodging place for travelers in the desert" [Jeremiah 9:2]. His visible distress over the adulteries of his fellow countrymen has led some to refer to him as "the weeping prophet."

Jeremiah never married, nor did he father any children [Jeremiah 16:2]. He lived a rather solitary existence, and his closest companion was probably his faithful scribe and secretary, Baruch. After the fall of Jerusalem in 586 B.C., he labored for a time with the survivors who were left behind in the holy city, and who had not been led away into captivity. Later he was called to minister among the Jews who had fled into Egypt. It was probably there that he died.

The basic theme of the prophetic book which bears his name is a series of stern warnings to the people of Judah to repent from their acts of spiritual adultery with the idolatrous pagans who lived about them, and to turn back to God. They were warned that should they refuse, they faced experiencing the same fate which befell their faithless sister Israel. After divorcing Israel, God had entered into a relationship with her sister Judah, but the latter was proving to be little better than the former. If a destruction of the covenant of marriage with God was to be avoided, Judah must exhibit some significant attitudinal and behavioral changes.

Declaring the guilt of His spouse, God said, "'If a man divorces his wife and she leaves him and marries another man, should he return to her again? Would not the land be completely defiled? But you have lived as a prostitute with many lovers — would you now return to Me?' declares the Lord. 'Look up to the barren heights and see. Is there any place where you have not been ravished? By the roadside you sat waiting for lovers, sat like a nomad in the desert. You have defiled the land with your prostitution and wickedness'" [Jeremiah 3:1-2]. God again referred back to a specific part of the Law of Moses

[Deuteronomy 24:1-4] which states that a husband who has divorced a wife because of her indecent behavior is not allowed to take her back again after she has gone and joined herself to another. This was a fact that Judah needed to seriously consider. If her indecent behavior was not checked, and quickly, she faced the possible irrevocable loss of her covenant relationship with God.

God had hoped that the example of her sister's spiritual folly, and His subsequent divorce from her, would be sobering enough to bring Judah to repentance. "'I thought that after she had done all this she would return to Me but she did not, and her unfaithful sister Judah saw it. I gave faithless Israel her certificate of divorce and sent her away because of all her adulteries. Yet I saw that her unfaithful sister Judah had no fear; she also went out and committed adultery. Because Israel's immorality mattered so little to her, she defiled the land and committed adultery with stone and wood. In spite of all this, her unfaithful sister Judah did not return to Me with all her heart, but only in pretense,' declares the Lord" [Jeremiah 3:7-10].

Although Judah made overtures at a return to God under the reforms of King Josiah, they were not truly heartfelt. It was a pretense; a sham; and God was not fooled. Because of her continued adulteries, God would eventually separate Himself from faithless Judah. This separation would last for many decades, spanning several generations of His people [Jeremiah 29:10-11], and would take the form, historically, of the Babylonian captivity.

Following this period of separation, God and Judah would again enter into a relationship with one another; one which, in some ways, would be far more satisfying and fruitful. From this union would come a Son: Jesus the Messiah. The offspring of the union of the northern kingdom of Israel, God's former spouse, with her pagan lovers would be a people known as the Samaritans. As John 4:9 clearly points out, the Jews and Samaritans, though closely related, had no association or dealings with one another. In part, this enmity could be traced back to the faithless behavior of the two mothers, Israel and Judah. One can only wonder how the pages of history in the Middle East might have been rewritten, perhaps more positively, had these two taken more seriously their covenants with their God!

It was never God's intention that either divorce or separation occur between Himself and His people. "'Return, faithless people,' declares the Lord, 'for I am your husband'" [Jeremiah 3:14]. God was desirous of a relationship, and, as with Israel, He was willing to show compassion and forgiveness to Judah, even though she was engaged in acts of gross immorality against Him, in order to achieve that desired goal. Even though "like a woman unfaithful to her husband, so you have been unfaithful to Me" [Jeremiah 3:20], nevertheless God was willing to welcome her back and restore the relationship if she would repent. "Return, faithless people," declares the Lord God, and "I will heal your faithlessness" [Jeremiah 3:22]. Israel, however, was unwilling to turn from her adulterous affairs, and Judah was only willing to return half-heartedly and under pretense. Thus, God *divorced* one and *separated* from the other.

These painful passages from the prophets Isaiah and Jeremiah have been the source of much confusion and debate down through the centuries. Some people, even after reading these declarations of Scripture, are simply unable or unwilling to accept the fact that the Lord God could ever have been personally involved in a divorce and remarriage. If, as some have staunchly maintained, these conditions constitute sin which is unpardonable, what does this suggest about our God?! Although it is certainly true that God was the innocent party in this whole tragic affair, one still cannot avoid the fact that God has been divorced and remarried! To state such is regarded as tantamount to sacrilege in some religious quarters; nonetheless, it is a truth irrefutably taught in the pages of Scripture. How tragic when personal biases and religious traditions blind one to truth, and to the unconditional acceptance of it.

Painful though it may be to acknowledge, one must accept the fact that God divorced His first wife Israel, and then married her sister Judah, from whom He later separated for a time. Through no fault of His own, the IDEAL was not even achieved by God Himself. Perhaps a greater awareness of this fact among God's people will provide them with a greater sensitivity and compassion as they come face to face with those who are experiencing similar relationship difficulties. Before one hastens to pass judgment and pronounce sentence against another who has experienced the dissolution of a covenant of marriage, one should exercise extreme caution lest the attitudes and actions displayed be an indirect expression of harsh judgment against God as well!

These passages from the prophets Isaiah and Jeremiah also assist in the clarification of another misconception commonly held: the view that God does not actually recognize a state of divorce, and that only death can terminate a marriage. If this be so, does this not suggest that God and Judah were guilty of an adulterous relationship?! If the first marriage was not truly at an end, because both spouses were still alive, then God was "living in sin" with the sister of His wife! Such accusations have often been hurled at one's fellow man, but would any man be so bold as to suggest such against God?! Perhaps reflection in this area will lead to greater caution in making such charges against others.

In many societies, the words divorce and remarriage carry with them some very negative connotations. Those to whom these words apply are viewed differently; often viewed as being somehow inferior or tainted. Heartless jokes and unfair assessments abound as to the moral integrity, or lack thereof, of those who have been through the trauma of marital breakdown. We are quick to label and libel such ones, but not always so quick to display concern or compassion, or to render some form of practical assistance. Extending a helping, healing hand to those who are down, in no way signifies approval of the *state* of divorce, or of any failure to achieve God's IDEAL. But, let us never assume that such disapproval thereby frees one from the need to demonstrate godly compassion.

Those who have dealt treacherously with a spouse need to be shown from God's Word just how far they have fallen from the glory of His IDEAL, and just how harmful their actions have been to themselves and to others. They must come to the conviction that they have sinned against both God and their families; they must be called to repentance, and, if possible, to reconcile or make restitution. Even though they may well be the "guilty party" in the breakdown of the relationship, they are not without hope, for they are not beyond the reach of God's forgiveness, or the cleansing power of Christ's blood. Rather than an attitude of cold condemnation, God's ambassadors of grace must show forth an attitude of loving concern, and proclaim a message of healing and hope.

THE PROPHET HOSEA

The topic of divorce and remarriage is discussed by only a quarter of the Minor Prophets, with the most extensive treatment being the prophetic work of Hosea.

Although not specifically stated in Scripture, it is commonly believed that Hosea was a native of the northern kingdom of Israel; possibly even a citizen of Samaria, since the ruler is referred to by this prophet as "our king" [Hosea 7:5].

Although little is known about his personal background, some scholars feel he may well have been a priest. It is also speculated that he might have come from a socially prominent family. Hosea was a contemporary of the prophet Isaiah, but their ministries each had a different focus. Whereas Isaiah was primarily concerned with the sins of Judah, Hosea's prophetic ministry was directed more toward the northern kingdom of Israel.

Based upon the following passage: "The word of the Lord that came to Hosea son of Beeri during the reigns of Uzziah, Jotham, Ahaz and Hezekiah, kings of Judah, and during the reign of Jeroboam son of Jehoash king of Israel" [Hosea 1:1], one can safely date his ministry from about 753 to 715 B.C. Thus, the book which bears his name is actually a compilation of various sermons and prophetic actions presented to the people of Israel over the course of several decades.

This was a time of complete chaos in the northern kingdom in almost all areas of life. The moral climate could only be characterized as corrupt in the extreme. The priests of God were in league with false prophets; worship of God had become a mockery; there was rebellion against all forms of constituted authority; politically the people were relying upon human defenses and foreign alliances rather than upon the power of their God. All of the Ten Commandments were being broken on a consistent basis throughout the nation. The people were destitute of knowledge of God, and "a spirit of prostitution" was so deeply ingrained within their hearts that they no longer acknowledged their God [Hosea 5:4]. In short, Israel, the bride of the Lord God, had chosen to engage in spiritual adultery and to turn away from her covenant of marriage.

The message of Hosea is simple and straightforward: Israel is the "chosen one" of God, and He who chose her is a loving, righteous, faithful Husband who is patiently hoping for a restored relationship with His straying bride. The relationship between God and Israel is emphasized as being a covenant involving mutual obligations and responsibilities. The message of Hosea is also one of inevitable doom for faithless Israel if she chooses not to repent and return to her Husband.

God, the loving Husband, longs for reconciliation with His unfaithful wife, ever hopeful of a restored relationship. But, God, the righteous Husband, realizes that a time of just reckoning must one day come. Due to His loving nature, this will be a painful moment for Him, but due to His righteous nature, it will be a necessary one. God is patient, not desiring any to experience the inevitable consequences of sin [2 Peter 3:9], but His patience has a limit. In the prophecy of Hosea one detects the day of national reckoning drawing nigh; one also detects the ever-hopeful rejected Husband longing for a reconciliation with His adulterous wife.

"When the Lord first spoke through Hosea, the Lord said to Hosea, 'Go, take to yourself a wife of harlotry, and have children of harlotry; for the land commits flagrant harlotry, forsaking the Lord'" [Hosea 1:2]. In obedience to his God, Hosea married Gomer the daughter of Diblaim. The relationship between these two was to be a visible representation to the people of Israel of their own tainted relationship with God. Just as Hosea, a righteous man, was married to a woman engaged in gross immorality, so also was God married to a "wife of harlotry." If the people of Israel were not willing to listen to the *words* of the prophets of God, then perhaps they would take note of the appalling *actions* of the prophets, and thus take to heart the object lesson being conveyed. This was the concept behind this methodology.

Because of the adulteries of Gomer, and of Israel, the relationship was for all intents and purposes not that of a husband and wife. "She is not my wife, and I am not her husband" [Hosea 2:2] is a statement which reflects quite well the attitudes of both Hosea and God as a result of the actions of their brides. Some have even seen this statement as a "divorce formula;" an official public declaration of the termination of a covenant of marriage. Whether "official" or not, the statement certainly conveys the harsh reality that a covenant of marriage had been destroyed by the faithless actions of one of the parties to it.

Hosea's relationship with Gomer was in serious trouble. A covenant with a spouse simply cannot be successfully maintained when one or both parties to that covenant are more concerned with pursuing other lovers, than together pursuing God's IDEAL. Both God and Hosea were forced to witness the tragic demise of their covenants of marriage because of the immoralities of their spouses.

The hope of the loving, faithful partner is that the unfaithful spouse will eventually reflect upon and realize the folly of their behavior, repent, and seek a restoration of the relationship. With Israel, the Lord even sought to "allure her" back to Him [Hosea 2:14], longing for the day when "you will call Me 'my husband'" again [vs. 16]. How God yearned to hear her say, "I will go back to my husband as at first, for then I was better off than now" [Hosea 2:7].

To visibly demonstrate His longing for that day, God instructed Hosea, "Go, show your love to your wife again, though she is loved by another and is an adulteress. Love her as the Lord loves the Israelites, though they turn to other gods and love the sacred raisin cakes" [Hosea 3:1]. In compliance with God's will, Hosea brought Gomer back to live with him, and charged her with these words, "You are to live with me many days; you must not be a prostitute or be intimate with any man, and I will live with you" [vs. 3]. This action by the prophet Hosea would demonstrate to the people of the land God's willingness to take them back as long as they were willing to live faithfully to their covenant and to cease playing the harlot.

It would be wonderful if history recorded that Hosea's visible warnings and encouragements had a positive effect on Israel. Sadly, they did not. Israel, unlike Gomer, refused to repent of her harlotries, and thus God was unable to take her back. The patience of God finally ran out, and He was forced to declare the relationship at an end. This sad fate is declared symbolically in the name of the daughter of Hosea and Gomer. "Gomer conceived again and gave birth to a daughter. Then the Lord said to Hosea, 'Call her Lo-Ruhamah (which means "not loved"), for I will no longer show love to the house of Israel, that I should at all forgive them. Yet I will show love to the house of Judah; and I will save them'" [Hosea 1:6-7]. God had been patient with Israel, giving her every opportunity to repent and return, but His bride was not to be swayed from her destructive course. Thus, God divorced her, and turned to her sister instead.

Some readers of this historical account are rather perplexed as to why God would command Hosea, a prophet and possibly a priest, to marry a prostitute. Wasn't this a violation of His Law? There is another possible interpretation, however, one far more consistent with the rest of biblical teaching. The key to interpreting the relationship between Hosea and Gomer is to remember that it was to be a visible parallel of the relationship between God and Israel. Thus, the latter would be reflected to a large extent in the former.

In light of God's relationship with Israel, it is likely that Hosea married a woman who later began engaging in adulterous activities, but who was not doing so when the marriage covenant was made. This was certainly what happened with God and Israel; she began to play the harlot much later. Thus, the phrase "wife of harlotry" may well be understood proleptically (i.e.: It was anticipatory, or even prophetic, in nature); God was looking forward to what Gomer would become, rather than to what she already was.

It is obvious from a study of the book of Hosea that, in spite of her eventual acts of adultery, God loved Israel very much and desired to win her back. He was willing to pursue her, allure her, and wait patiently for her; but, Israel was left unmoved by His affectionate advances. Her heart had become hardened as her immoralities increased. In time, God had no choice but to send her away and turn His attentions to another.

On a level much deeper than the story of a prophet and his wayward wife, this is a message of spurned divine love and unrealized hope. In this account, the pain of God over a destroyed relationship is deeply felt; a pain which should motivate men to strive all the more to live faithfully to Him, seeking after the IDEAL in all of life's interpersonal relationships.

THE PROPHET MICAH

Another prophet who was a contemporary of Isaiah and Hosea was Micah, a man from the town of Moresheth, which was located about 25 miles southwest of Jerusalem. Nothing is known about his family or home life, but, like Amos, another contemporary who lived just 17 miles away, Micah was a man of the country, possibly of very humble origins.

Micah was not nearly as much concerned about political reformation, unlike some of the other prophets, as he was the religious and moral abuses which were rampant in the land. The poorer working classes were being mercilessly exploited by the rich. Injustices prevailed on every hand, rulers and judges could be bought for a bribe, the concept of ethics was seemingly unheard of, and corrupt business practices abounded. Society was on the verge of a complete moral collapse.

Religiously, the situation was no better. The prophets and priests were only interested in how much money they could obtain for their services [Micah 3:11], and false teachers were numerous. Micah portrayed the character of the nation well when he stated, rather sarcastically, that if a false prophet were to come to the people of Judah and proclaim, "'I will prophesy for you plenty of wine and beer,' he would be just the prophet for this people!" [Micah 2:11].

The people were indeed "religious," but it was a hollow religion; little more than a heartless, lifeless performance of ritual; a cold ceremonialism devoid of spirit. They mistakenly assumed, not unlike many today, that by correct observance of the externals of religion one could thereby stand approved before God. Right rituals, however, have never been the basis of right relationship with God. God looks to the heart!

Micah sought to convey to the people God's desire for compassion over sacrifice, social justice over burnt offerings, personal holiness and spirituality over the worthless sham of perpetuating religious rituals with hearts focused on self rather than on God. The Lord sought a people more concerned with following the *spirit* of the Law, than the *letter* of the Law, and with spirituality, than with legalism. "He has showed you, O man, what is good. And what does the Lord require of you? To act justly and to love mercy and to walk humbly with your God" [Micah 6:8].

Within the context of this discussion of spirituality and social justice, one finds the following passage: "You drive the women of My people from their pleasant homes. You take away My blessing from their children forever" [Micah 2:9]. There is some disagreement among scholars as to exactly what is being conveyed in this statement. It is felt by some that the driving away of women from their homes may be a reference to divorce; others feel that this may be reading too much into the text.

One logical interpretation would be that this is a reference to heartless rulers casting women and children out of their homes in order to possess their property. Such practices were indeed occurring at that time among the people of God. There is also no question but what God was strongly opposed to such.

If this passage *does* focus on the plight of the divorced, however, one discovers yet again the deep concern of the Lord for those who are victims of the cruelty and treachery of ungodly spouses. The moral climate of society had degenerated to the point where heartless husbands were evicting their wives and children from the home, leaving them in the streets in a state of destitution. Some would even refuse to issue the wife a certificate of divorce, thus forbidding her the legal right to enter a supportive relationship with another. This behavior was typical of a wide variety of social injustices occurring at that time among the Jewish people.

It is highly probable that God is displaying in this passage His displeasure over the cruelty being manifested by certain heartless husbands toward their wives and children. The covenant people of God needed to begin demonstrating once again a spirit of compassion toward one another; a fact which was especially true in the context of their marital relationships.

THE PROPHET MALACHI

The final book in the Old Testament canon, and the last of the twelve men designated as Minor Prophets, is Malachi. Jewish tradition states he was a member of the Great Synagogue, was from the tribe of Zebulun, and that he died young. Aside from these ancient traditions, nothing further is known of the personal background of this prophet of God.

By an examination of various internal aspects of the book which bears his name, one can date this work fairly accurately during the time of the reforms of Ezra and Nehemiah. A date around 435 B.C. for the prophecies of Malachi would not be too far off.

One of the major concerns of Malachi was that the men of Israel, following their return from Babylonian Captivity, were not honoring their covenants of marriage with their wives. No longer was the IDEAL being sought in their interpersonal relationships. For these failings, God, through His prophet, issued a stern warning: "The Lord has been a witness between you and the wife of your youth, against whom you have dealt treacherously, though she is your companion and your wife by covenant. But not one has done so who has a remnant of the Spirit ... Take heed, then, to your spirit, and let no one deal treacherously against the wife of your youth. 'For I hate divorce,' says the Lord, the God of Israel, 'and him who covers his garment with wrong,' says the Lord of hosts. 'So take heed to your spirit, that you do not deal treacherously'" [Malachi 2:14-16].

Malachi displays the truth that marriage is a "covenant" between two people; a covenant to which God is a witness. Additionally, God is a witness to how the parties to this covenant behave toward one another. Those who deal treacherously with their covenant mates are demonstrating, for both God and man to witness, they do not even have a remnant of the Spirit dwelling within them.

The people of God were being called to carefully examine their hearts. What manner of spirit were they displaying toward their spouses? If it was a treacherous spirit, they needed a radical transformation of heart. God hates divorce! So should His people. By perceiving marital breakdowns in the same light as God, perhaps one would apply himself all the more to achieving the IDEAL.

"'I hate divorce,' says the Lord, the God of Israel." There is probably no better statement with which to close the teachings of the Old Testament canon on the subject of man's failure to achieve the IDEAL for marriage. God's feelings about divorce are clearly stated. He abhors it! This should be forever imprinted upon the minds of His people.

The writings of the Old Testament nowhere deny the reality of marital breakdown. Indeed, it is depicted as occurring all too frequently. Even God Himself was a victim of it. Relationships end, and others are entered into. This is a reality which the Bible clearly acknowledges. In response, God has even issued specific laws designed to lessen the impact of the crueler aspects of this tragic reality. Nevertheless, it is vital to note that simply because God recognizes the fact of man's frequent failure to achieve His IDEAL, and makes provisions to lessen the effects of such upon the innocent victims, does not thereby demonstrate His approval of the state of divorce itself. Yes, divorce is a reality of which God is painfully aware, but another reality with which man must be aware is God's hatred of it!

An understanding of Old Testament law, history, poetry and prophecy, with respect to this topic, is an essential preparatory and foundational stage for fully grasping the insights to be conveyed in the writings of the New Testament. The teachings of Jesus and Paul, who made repeated references back to these truths, will never be completely understood without a knowledge of the foundation upon which those doctrines are built.

Chapter 4
Examination of Key Greek Words

The New Testament documents were originally written in the Greek language, although Aramaic and Hebraic influences upon the text are clearly evident. To gain deeper insight into the meaning of specific passages and to facilitate correct interpretation, therefore, one must carefully examine in the original language significant words and phrases relevant to the subject matter being studied.

Although most translations do an excellent job of rendering the original language text into English, none of them can lay claim to being flawless. On many occasions they are simply unable to convey the depth and diversity of meaning that is inherent within the source language. It is a simple fact of translation that not all of what is conveyed in the original carries over to the second language. This is especially true with the significance of verb forms, many of which are absolutely critical to a correct understanding of particular passages in the New Testament documents. When a translator fails to convey the true meaning of a particular verb form in a certain text, the result may well be a major alteration of the message the inspired writer sought to communicate. Such deviation, even though unintentional, may be significant enough to promote confusion or even false doctrine.

An understanding of the words and forms utilized by the original authors of Scripture, therefore, is vital in some areas of doctrinal interpretation. This is especially true with regard to the teachings of the Lord on divorce and remarriage.

The Greek language has one of the longest and most fully documented histories of all the languages of the European continent. It can be traced back over 3500 years through several significant developmental phases. The period of greatest interest to the biblical student, however, is the Hellenistic Period, also known as the Koine

Period, which extended from about 300 B.C. to 500 A.D.

In the year 336 B.C., when only 20 years old, Alexander the Great (356 - 323 B.C.) ascended to the throne of his slain father, Philip of Macedon. During the remaining 13 years of his brief life he would leave an indelible mark upon the history of mankind. Although a great military leader and strategist, his single most lasting accomplishment, historically speaking, was his introduction of the Greek culture and language to the peoples he conquered.

Though a Macedonian by birth, Alexander loved the Greek way of life, and set about promoting it with a missionary fervor. He received a classical education, studying under Aristotle himself. On his many campaigns he carried copies of the *Iliad* and the *Odyssey*, which he read repeatedly. It was reported that every night he slept with a copy of the *Iliad* and a dagger under his pillow. Knowledge and conquest were his life.

In every area of the world which he and his army conquered, Alexander commanded the Greek language be taught to the people. It was his unwavering desire for Greek to become the official language of the empire. In an effort to achieve that goal, Alexander became Hellenism's greatest apostle and missionary.

His dream was largely realized, and by the time of the first century A.D., during which the New Testament documents were penned, Greek had become the common language utilized throughout the Roman Empire, hence the designation "koine," which means "common." The fact that this language was common to all parts of the empire made it the natural choice for the transmission of the Good News in written form. The disciples of Christ were commissioned to spread the Gospel "to the ends of the earth" [Acts 1:8], and to "make disciples of all nations" [Matthew 28:19]. What better vehicle to accomplish this noble task than the Greek language.

The inspired writers of the New Testament documents penned their message of saving grace in the common, ordinary language of the masses; a vehicle so designed that even those without formal education could readily grasp the Truths being proclaimed.

A great many centuries have passed, however, since those original documents (the "autographs") were written, and radical changes have occurred between the social perceptions and practices of that time and ours. Additionally, those autographs (none of which are now in existence) have been copied and recopied, translated and retranslated, paraphrased and revised to the point where the exact intent of the authors is occasionally obscured from the modern mind. Thus the need, in any serious study of these New Testament writings, to employ a hermeneutic which seeks to do far more than bolster one's biases or traditional perceptions through proof-texting, but which seeks instead to honestly perceive and receive the message as it would have been understood by the original recipients. Such a process must take into account not only their customs, laws, history, religion, and other key aspects of their life, but also their language.

The language of the Greeks was/is one of the most precise and expressive known to man. Each word may have numerous nuances and shades of meaning, all of which can be easily lost in translation. A single concept might well be expressed by the use of dozens of different Greek words, each providing a slightly different insight or perspective. Further, when it comes to the interpretation of the Greek verbs, one simply cannot state strongly enough how vital it is to solid, sound exegesis that the translator and interpreter pay very careful attention to the forms (tense, voice, mood, person, number). Each Greek verb can employ scores of varying forms, each portraying some thought or action from a different perspective. It is no overstatement to suggest that to fail to correctly identify the verb forms often results in a failure to correctly interpret the meaning of the passage. This will be seen to be especially true with reference to the teachings of Jesus on divorce and remarriage.

Within the pages of the Greek New Testament there are five basic words employed by the authors to convey the concept of divorce. Within the Greek Old Testament (the *Septuagint*) there are three additional words utilized. A basic familiarity with them will shed further light on the teachings of Jesus and Paul with respect to this topic.

APOLUO — This verb is a compound of two separate Greek words: "apo," which is a preposition meaning "from, away from," and "luo," a verb which conveys the idea of "loosing, releasing, setting free." When combined to form "apoluo," the concept of "releasing from, setting free, liberating, sending away, dismissing, and loosing from" is communicated. Thus, this word, which appears 69 times within the pages of the New Testament writings, clearly indicates an unbinding of that which was previously joined.

In Matthew 27:26 Pilate "released Barabbas" to the crowd which was demanding the crucifixion of Christ Jesus. This "notorious prisoner" had formerly been a man held in strict confinement, perhaps chained to a wall in a dark, damp prison cell. His condition seemed hopeless; his prospects for freedom virtually nil. However, when Pilate "released" him, his condition changed dramatically; he was loosed, set free, liberated; his bondage had been terminated.

In a marriage relationship, the husband and wife are bound to one another. A union between two people has occurred; they have become one flesh [Genesis 2:24]. When that sacred union is broken, however, by one or both parties to this covenant of marriage, there transpires an untying or loosing of that which was previously joined. When a husband gives his wife a certificate of divorce, he publicly and officially declares her to be released, not only from the relationship, but also from his authority. She has been sent away, set free, liberated.

With the sole exception of Hebrews 13:23, which speaks of the release of Timothy from prison, "apoluo" is found exclusively in the four Gospels [Matthew, Mark, Luke, John] and in the book of Acts. It is utilized by the inspired writers to signify the breakdown of a marital relationship in the following passages: Matthew 1:19; 5:31-32; 19:3,7,8,9; Mark 10:2,4,11,12; and Luke 16:18. In the Greek Old Testament it is used in the Exodus 21 passage.

APOSTASION — Like the previous word, "apostasion" is a compound formed by the joining of two separate Greek words. The preposition "apo" (from, away from) is added as a prefix to "stasis," which means "a standing, a state, existence." It imparts to the reader

DOWN, BUT NOT OUT

the idea of "standing off from" someone or something. When used with reference to the state of marriage, it bespeaks a state of existence in which there is a "standing away from" one another. The "one flesh" state of being that existed between a man and woman is now severed; their lives are no longer intertwined; they have parted company, and each stands separately and apart from the other.

Generally, "apostasion" is used in conjunction with the word "biblion" (scroll, document, certificate), and the resultant phrase is most often translated "certificate of divorce." This was an official document signifying the termination of a covenant of marriage between a husband and wife. From a legal perspective, they would thereafter be recognized as existing in a state separate and apart from one another; a state of union was no longer regarded as existing.

This particular word appears only 3 times within the pages of the New Testament documents [Matthew 5:31; 19:7; Mark 10:4]. In the *Septuagint* it can be found in Deuteronomy 24:3,5; Isaiah 50:1; and Jeremiah 3:8.

LUSIS — This term is derived from the root word "luo" (see above), and means to be "loosed, freed, released" from any kind of bond or connection. It can be located in only one passage in the New Testament writings: "Are you bound to a wife? Do not seek to be released ("lusis"). Are you released ("luo") from a wife? Do not seek a wife" [1 Corinthians 7:27]. As with the words examined previously, this clearly denotes an unbinding or severing of the marriage union.

APHIEMI — This word is used quite extensively within the New Covenant Scriptures, appearing some 146 times (only 14 of which are found outside of the four Gospels). It is used quite infrequently, however, with reference to divorce: occurring only 3 times, all of which are in a single passage [1 Corinthians 7:11,12,13].

"Aphiemi" is a verb which means "to desert or forsake, abandon, dismiss, send away, leave alone or behind." Utilizing this word, Paul wrote of men who "abandoned natural relations with women and were inflamed with lust for one another" [Romans 1:27]. Jesus, through His servant John, made this grave evaluation of the church at Ephesus, "You have forsaken your first love" [Revelation 2:4].

In a covenant of marriage, some spouses do indeed "abandon" their mates, and in effect "forsake" their first love. The despicable dealings in view in this particular Greek word are desertion and abandonment of a covenant mate.

CHORIZO — This verb appears 13 times in the New Testament documents, 5 of which have reference to divorce [Matthew 19:6; Mark 10:9; 1 Corinthians 7:10,11,15]. It signifies "to sever, disunite, put asunder, divide, separate." The apostle Paul, in his epistle to the church in Rome, twice uses it to proclaim the positive message of Christ's faithfulness to His bride and God's faithfulness to His covenant: "Who shall separate us from the love of Christ? Shall trouble or hardship or persecution or famine or nakedness or danger or sword?" [Romans 8:35]. Paul avows his conviction that nothing in all of creation "will be able to separate us from the love of God that is in Christ Jesus our Lord" [vs. 39]. Paul has given us a glimpse of the IDEAL. The Lord is deeply committed to His relationship with mankind; He will remain loyal to His covenant regardless of the challenges that may threaten to sever that blessed union. If only more spouses had that same resolve! Tragically, it often takes far less of a challenge to separate husbands and wives from one another, and to put asunder their covenant of marriage.

Within the pages of the Greek Old Testament, one finds three additional words which shed light on the concept of divorce as perceived in the biblical documents. They are as follows:

ENKATALEIPO — This compound Greek verb is formed out of three separate words: (1) the preposition "en" which is generally translated "in," (2) "kata," also a preposition, meaning "down, down from," and (3) the verb "leipo," which means "to leave behind, forsake, to leave destitute or lacking."

"Enkataleipo" thus signifies an abandoning of someone; to leave another in dire straits, or to leave them in a helpless, hopeless condition.

In the ancient world depicted within the pages of the Bible, a divorce between a husband and wife often resulted in the latter being left destitute. To be utterly forsaken; to be cast down and left defenseless; is the significance of "enkataleipo." It was for this reason, and because of His tremendous compassion for those being so victimized, that God issued some of the previously discussed laws that have been preserved within the Pentateuch.

This particular word is found in the Malachi 2 passage, and with the substance of its meaning in mind, verses 14-16 take on heightened significance: "The Lord has been a witness between you and the wife of your youth, against whom you have dealt treacherously, though she is your companion and your wife by covenant. But not one has done so who has a remnant of the Spirit ... Take heed, then, to your spirit, and let no one deal treacherously against the wife of your youth. 'For I hate divorce,' says the Lord, the God of Israel, 'and him who covers his garment with wrong,' says the Lord of hosts. 'So take heed to your spirit, that you do not deal treacherously.'"

The phrase "deal treacherously" is the attempt of the *New American Standard Bible* to render the word "enkataleipo." Certainly, one would have to agree that to abandon one's covenant companion to destitution through an act of unjustified divorce is about as treacherous an act as one can commit. The Lord states that when husbands abuse their wives in this way, or when they deal with anyone in a treacherous manner, they profane the covenant of their fathers [Malachi 2:10]. Thus, they stand condemned as covenant breakers, having broken covenant not only with their wives, but also with their fellow man and with their God.

"Enkataleipo" also appears within the pages of the New Testament, but in its 9 occurrences is never used with reference to divorce. It is used in some rather emotionally charged passages, however, which clearly illustrate the depth of meaning this word conveys. Jesus cried out from the cross, "My God, My God, why have You forsaken Me?" [Matthew 27:46; Mark 15:34]. In his final epistle before his execution, Paul wrote the young evangelist Timothy, "Demas ... has deserted me" [2 Timothy 4:10]. A few verses later he wrote, "At my first defense, no one came to my support, but everyone deserted me" [vs. 16]. To be left

AL MAXEY

destitute of support from those you believed to be your closest companions and greatest supporters is a deeply traumatizing experience. Certainly, both Paul and Jesus could comprehend and empathize with the painful plight of women who had been abandoned, deserted or forsaken.

EXAPOSTELLO — This word is found in the Deuteronomy passages; also in Isaiah 50:1, Jeremiah 3:1,8 and Malachi 2:16. It, like the previous word, is a verb formed by the combination of three separate Greek words: (1) "ek," which is a preposition meaning "from out of," (2) "apo," another preposition, signifying "from, away from," and (3) "stello," a verb which means "to keep away, stand aloof from or avoid someone." When these three are combined into one word, it usually conveys the idea of getting rid of someone, sending them away so as to remove them from one's presence.

The word "apostle" is a form of this same word and signifies one who has been sent forth, usually with a specific message to proclaim. In like manner, "exapostello" denotes one who is sent forth from the presence of another, also with a message accompanying that departure; in this case, however, that message is *not* "good news." The message the sent away spouse carries with him or her is, "You are not wanted, you are not needed, you are not loved. Depart from my presence."

This word further portrays a sending forth of someone from out of one condition, or state of existence, into another. In the context of this study that would be the sending forth of a spouse from out of the state of marriage into a state of divorce. This put away spouse is also being sent forth with a very clear message from the one initiating the divorce, a message conveyed in the meaning of each of the three parts of this word: "From out of" ... "Away from" ... "Keep aloof from, avoid." It is a negative message; one of termination; a declaration of dissolution. It is a proclamation of one's desire to have absolutely no further relationship with the one being cast off.

"Exapostello" appears 11 times within the pages of the New Testament documents, but never with reference to divorce. In the Lord's Parable of the Tenants [Luke 20:9-16], however, this word is

88

twice used to clearly convey the same hurtful message of "go away, you're not wanted here" to the owner of the vineyard and his servants.

The ancient Jews, therefore, were not only dealing treacherously with the wives of their youth, their covenant partners for life, but they were also adding cruelty to the list of sins committed against their spouses; a cruelty conveyed through a heartless, hurtful message of utter rejection.

EKBALLO — Found in the Leviticus passages, in Ezra 10, and in Ezekiel 44:22, this word occurs quite frequently in the New Testament (82 times), but never with reference to divorce. It is a verb composed of the preposition "ek" ("from out of") and the verb "ballo," which means "to throw or cast." Thus, "ekballo" signifies a "throwing out" or a "casting out." Occasionally, one will hear a heartless spouse speak of "throwing their wife/husband out!" Such is the import of this word.

Within the pages of the New Testament it is generally the term used to depict the casting out of demons. The unholy union of demon and host-body was terminated; a relationship severed via the casting out process. The same is true with respect to divorce. The two, who became "one flesh" in a holy union, are now two once again. A "casting out" has taken place.

It should be abundantly clear, to even a casual observer, that the words utilized by the inspired writers of Scripture convey, both individually and collectively, the reality of terminated relationships, often accompanied by some degree of animosity, bitterness and even cruelty on the part of one or both of the spouses. These are not pleasant word pictures; they describe human nature at its worst. But, ugly and uncomfortable though it may be to behold, they do depict a basic reality of mankind's existence in this world: men and women often fail to achieve, or even seek to acquire, God's IDEAL for the marriage relationship, and when that occurs people are harmed and left hurting.

Further, absolutely none of the words used in Scripture with reference to this subject convey the false notion that the relationships being described are just "marriages on hold," and thus not really divorces at all. These words clearly depict the total, and often irrevocable, dissolution of a covenant of marriage. To insist, as do some, that God does not actually recognize the end of a marriage, save by the death of one or both of the covenant partners, is to thoroughly misunderstand and misapply the truths of God's Word. Additionally, it is to fail to perceive the meaning of the words selected by the Spirit, and conveyed to the writers of the original documents, which convey those truths. Jesus told the Sadducees, who were confused over a particular concept concerning marriage, "You are in error because you do not know the Scriptures" [Matthew 22:29]. That is also the cause of the confusion of many today.

The specific words chosen by God to convey His message to mankind were not selected randomly or carelessly, rather "men spoke from God as they were carried along by the Holy Spirit" [2 Peter 1:21]. Since "all Scripture is God-breathed" [2 Timothy 3:16], it behooves the reader to pay very careful attention not only to what is being said, but also to how it is being said. The words utilized in the original text of the Scriptures, and the various forms in which those words appear, will greatly assist the student of God's Word in understanding His will. It will soon be displayed just how true this is with respect to the subject of divorce and remarriage.

Chapter 5
The Testimony of the Gospel Records

Turning one's attention to the four New Testament documents known collectively as the Gospels, the discovery is quickly made that the bulk of the Lord's teaching on divorce and remarriage is contained within the Synoptic Gospels (Matthew, Mark, Luke). The term synoptic means to "view together," and signifies a "common point-of-view." The first three Gospel accounts, in general, follow a very similar pattern and share a similar focus as they examine the life and teachings of Jesus Christ. John's record, however, is very much dissimilar to the other three in focus, emphasis and scope. Thus, it is excluded by scholars from the synoptic grouping.

Although each of the inspired synoptic writers present the teachings of Jesus on the subject of this study, only Matthew does so extensively. Thus, the vast majority of our understanding of Jesus' perspective of this vital issue is found within the pages of the first book of the New Testament canon. The writings of Mark and Luke serve to supplement that information, and heighten one's awareness, in a few vital areas.

Before an in-depth study of the specifics of the Lord's teaching on divorce and remarriage (which will follow in the next chapter), it would be beneficial to examine each of the passages contained in the Gospel records for the purpose of placing them within their proper historical, cultural, and theological context. Perceiving the pertinent background information about a passage is often critical in properly interpreting that passage. Any hermeneutic which fails to do so is suspect, and any position promoted from such shallow study should be viewed with suspicion. The statements of Jesus were not given in a vacuum, but rather reflect an intimate association with, and cognizance of, His times. Only by an awareness of those times can one fully expect to appreciate the depth of His teaching on this subject.

The Gospel of Matthew

As one begins a survey of the Gospel records, an encounter with a young couple named Joseph and Mary soon occurs. These two were "betrothed" to one another, or "pledged to be married" [Matthew 1:18]. Although some have equated this state of betrothal with the more modern period of engagement, the two actually are quite dissimilar. To the mind of the ancient Jew, a betrothal was perceived as being far more binding than the engagements of this day and age.

In the presence of witnesses, the terms of the marriage were jointly accepted. God's blessing was formally pronounced upon the union. From that moment forward, the two were regarded as husband and wife, although they would not yet live together, nor would the marriage be consummated through sexual union. A covenant had been entered into between the man and woman, nevertheless certain privileges and responsibilities associated with that covenant were reserved for future fulfillment.

During the betrothal, sexual infidelity constituted a far more serious offense than a mere act of fornication. It was a violation of a sacred covenant between a man and woman. In the presence of God they had vowed to one another to remain pure and chaste until the time of the wedding festivities. A breach of promise carried with it severe consequences for the faithless party, up to and including death. Termination of a state of betrothal, regardless of the cause, was regarded as equivalent to a divorce.

The church, which is the bride of Christ, is presently in the betrothal phase of her relationship with the Bridegroom, awaiting the great eternal wedding feast that will one day occur when the Lord returns to claim His bride and take her home to live with Him. As His betrothed, she has an obligation to keep herself pure and chaste [Ephesians 5:25-27]. The apostle Paul wrote, "I am jealous for you with a godly jealousy.

I promised you to one husband, to Christ, so that I might present you as a pure virgin to Him" [2 Corinthians 11:2]. In the next verse, Paul shared one of his greatest concerns: that the betrothed of Christ, His church, might at some point be seduced away from the purity and sincerity of her devotion to the Bridegroom. Should the bride of Christ defile herself with worldly lovers during this time of preparation for the wedding festivities, the result could well be an eternal separation from the Groom.

With this background information in mind, Joseph and Mary are presented in Scripture as betrothed to be married, "but before they came together (i.e.: before they had sexual relations with one another), she was found to be with child" [Matthew 1:18]. Although the passage goes on to explain she was with child "through the Holy Spirit," Joseph did not immediately possess this information. Initially, his assessment of the situation was very basic and incontrovertible: Mary was pregnant and he was not the father. What other possible conclusion could be drawn than his beloved had been unfaithful to her vows, to him, and to her God? One can only imagine the hurt and confusion this situation must have generated within the heart of Joseph.

Being a righteous man, it would not have been proper for him to marry a woman impregnated by another man during their betrothal. Therefore, Joseph "had in mind to divorce her quietly" [Matthew 1:19]. Decades later the apostle Paul would write, "what do righteousness and wickedness have in common?" [2 Corinthians 6:14]. Undoubtedly, Joseph, like Paul, understood that those desiring to live righteously before their God could not be yoked together with those who willfully transgressed His Law. Mary's unexpected pregnancy certainly seemed to indicate that she did not share Joseph's righteous resolve. Therefore, the latter deemed it necessary to dissolve the union.

Joseph, being a righteous man, faced this distressing situation in a most admirable manner. It was his determination to "divorce her quietly." Had Joseph's character been less godly, he could easily have publicly shamed and defamed his seemingly faithless bride-to-be. After all, he might well reason, had she not brought shame and disgrace upon him by her sexual infidelity and her subsequent pregnancy? Why should he not display the same lack of concern for her that she had seemingly displayed for him? It was even within Joseph's legal right to demand that Mary be stoned to death for her sin against him [Leviticus 20:10; Deuteronomy 22:22; John 8:3-5].

Instead of exacting vengeance, or returning hurt for hurt, Joseph determined to simply end the relationship quickly and quietly. According to one translation, his resolve was to "put her away secretly." Why was Joseph so intent upon keeping this matter private? Because "he did not want to expose her to public disgrace" [Matthew 1:19]. This insight into the heart of Joseph comes from the Greek word "deigmatizo," a word used only here and in Colossians 2:15, which means "to make a public example or spectacle of." Even though Mary had seemingly violated their covenant and betrayed his faith in her, Joseph was simply unwilling to inflict a harsh retribution upon her in return. Such was the abundant nature of his love for her!

Joseph realized Mary's apparent unfaithfulness made it impossible for him, being a righteous man, to proceed with the upcoming wedding festivities. The betrothal would have to be terminated; a divorce would have to be sought. Nevertheless, his deep devotion to her made cruel, harsh, retributive actions inconceivable on his part. This attitude of heart speaks volumes about this great man of faith; a man who would soon become a godly example to the young Jesus during His early, formative years. God had certainly chosen the earthly father-figure for His Son well, for in this humble carpenter we truly catch a glimpse of a heart focused upon the IDEAL in interpersonal relationships.

Although the future looked bleak for this young couple, Scripture records a much brighter outcome than at first seemed inevitable. The divorce, of course, never occurred, for "an angel of the Lord appeared to him in a dream and said, 'Joseph son of David, do not be afraid to take Mary home as your wife, because what is conceived in her is from the Holy Spirit. She will give birth to a son, and you are to give Him the name Jesus, because He will save His people from their sins.' When Joseph woke up, he did what the angel of the Lord had commanded him and took Mary home as his wife. But he had no union with her until she gave birth to a son. And he gave Him the name Jesus" [Matthew

1:20-21, 24-25].

Several great lessons are taught in the account of the relationship between Joseph and Mary. Clearly conveyed is the truth that God desires His people to live lives of righteousness, and to contemplate a life-long union with one not equally devoted to the pursuit of such a lifestyle would be to invite disaster. In the case before us, Mary was not actually guilty of the indiscretion of which Joseph suspected her. Had she been, however, he would have been entirely justified in terminating the relationship; indeed, it would be the only option of a righteous man. Although God takes no pleasure in divorce, He takes even less delight in His people joining themselves together with those whose hearts are committed to the world, and whose actions are characterized by carnality.

Another vital lesson learned from this series of events in the lives of Joseph and Mary is the importance of carefully examining all aspects of a situation prior to passing judgment or taking action. There is little question but what a significant number of marriages have ended due to a lack of investigation and communication, and the resultant conclusions falsely reached. The "truth of the matter" often seems so obvious; one's assumptions so valid; until the parties involved take the time to genuinely communicate with one another.

It took an act of communication to salvage the relationship between Joseph and Mary; a revelation from God that the reality was far different from the appearance. In the centuries since, communication still remains one of the most effective tools for resolving troubled relationships. Situations aren't always as they seem; the reality many times eludes us. Our covenant relationships are much too precious to cast aside due to assumptions acquired without investigation or communication. What a tragedy it would have been for Joseph and Mary, and for all of mankind, had Joseph acted on his assumptions without the benefit of additional information.

Further, we learn from this historical event that even should a divorce prove necessary, one is not thereby given license to act cruelly and vindictively toward the guilty party. Joseph certainly appeared to be the innocent, injured party in this situation, but he refused to display anything other than a charitable, merciful spirit. To inflict injury upon another, simply because one has been injured by them, falls far short of the example and nature of God. Joseph reflected the heart of the Lord in his proposed resolution of his relationship difficulties with Mary; in so doing, he serves as a shining beacon to mankind.

Three decades pass before one encounters the next reference to divorce and remarriage. Jesus had entered the public phase of His ministry to mankind, and was delivering a moving series of messages which have since come to be known collectively as the Sermon on the Mount [Matthew 5-7]. All through this discourse with His disciples, Jesus displayed the concept of living up to the IDEAL in virtually every area of one's life, with special emphasis upon one's interpersonal relationships. This body of instruction constitutes the very core and essence of the teachings of Jesus Christ, dealing with ethical, moral and spiritual issues of fundamental import unto every age of humanity.

If one examines the Lord's Sermon on the Mount carefully, it will quickly become apparent that the major theme of the messages is: interpersonal relationships. The way in which men relate to their God, to the things of this world, to those who love them, as well as to those who don't, and even how one relates to himself, are all covered clearly and concisely by Christ Jesus. It is a call to deeper spirituality and nobler conduct in every area of one's life. Jesus repeatedly referred His disciples to the Law of Moses, and then challenged them to even greater spiritual commitment.

In the Law it was commanded, "Thou shalt not commit murder," but Jesus taught that one must not even be angry with a brother [Matthew 5:21-22]. Well over sixty years later, with these very words undoubtedly in mind, the aged apostle John wrote, "Anyone who hates his brother is a murderer, and you know that no murderer has eternal life in him" [1 John 3:15].

The Law taught it was wrong to commit adultery. Jesus, however, challenged His listeners to an even deeper application: to look lustfully upon another was also to be regarded as sinful [Matthew 5:27-28]. Restraining oneself from committing the physical act of sexual infidelity with another, although good in and of itself, was not sufficient to absolve one of guilt if the act was committed within the heart and mind.

"You have heard that it was said, 'Love your neighbor and hate your enemy.' But I tell you: love your enemies and pray for those who persecute you, that you may be sons of your Father in heaven. Be perfect, therefore, as your heavenly Father is perfect" [Matthew 5:43-45, 48]. The challenge of the Lord is: develop and maintain a spirituality and maturity that transcends and transforms the world about you. Strive for the IDEAL in all of your interpersonal relationships; in so doing, demonstrate the reality of your relationship with the Father, and, by your life, call others to experience the same.

Within the context of this discussion, one comes across the first statement of Jesus with reference to divorce and remarriage. "It has been said, 'Anyone who divorces his wife must give her a certificate of divorce.' But I tell you that anyone who divorces his wife, except for marital unfaithfulness, causes her to become an adulteress, and anyone who marries the divorced woman commits adultery" [Matthew 5:31-32].

At first reading, this certainly appears to be a clear-cut, well-defined statement; no shades of gray; solidly black and white with regard to interpretation. That this is *not* the case, and the facts which validate that assessment, will be amply displayed as the intent and specifics of the Lord's teaching is examined in much greater depth in the following chapter. At this point in the study, it must suffice to simply place the statement itself, without comment, within its historical, biblical, and theological context.

Following His transfiguration, but prior to His triumphal entry into the city of Jerusalem, Jesus "left Galilee and went into the region of Judea to the other side of the Jordan" [Matthew 19:1]. It is the understanding of many scholars, from a close examination of this passage and its parallel in Mark 10:1, that Jesus left Galilee with the city of Jerusalem in Judea as His destination, but that He traveled through the region of Perea, which was across the Jordan from Judea, so as to avoid passing through the hostile territory of Samaria. Thus, it is very likely that our Lord's next statement on divorce and remarriage occurred in the tetrarchy of Herod Antipas. If this was the case, and there is good evidence that it was, this would prove to be an extremely significant factor in helping one to understand the questions addressed to Jesus at that particular time.

Herod Antipas, who reigned from 4 B.C. to 39 A.D., was an unusually immoral, crafty, and inhumane ruler. It was to this man that Pilate sent Jesus following His arrest, at which time Herod "ridiculed and mocked Him," dressed Him up in an elegant robe, and then sent Him back to Pilate for crucifixion [Luke 23:11]. In the summer of 39 A.D., Herod Antipas was banished by the Roman Emperor Caligula to Lyons, in Gaul, where, according to the ancient Jewish historian Josephus, he died in great misery.

It was also Herod Antipas who was responsible for having John, the forerunner of the Messiah, beheaded [Matthew 14:1-12; Mark 6:14-29; Luke 3:19-20]. John was arrested because he was condemning Herod for his marriage to Herodias, saying, "It is not lawful for you to have your brother's wife" [Mark 6:18]. Herod had divorced his Nabatean wife in order to marry Herodias, whom he had taken away from his brother Herod Philip. This was in violation of the Law of Moses, which specifically stated, "Do not have sexual relations with your brother's wife; that would dishonor your brother" [Leviticus 18:16].

Herodias herself was also infamous for her incestuous marital relationships. She was first married to her step-brother, by whom she had a daughter, Salome. Later, she entered into a marriage with her uncle, Philip; then into a third marriage with Philip's brother, Herod Antipas. Following in the footsteps of her mother, Salome also broke with what was widely considered to be acceptable behavior in Jewish culture by openly renouncing her marriage vows. This incident is reported by Josephus in *Antiquities of the Jews* [book 15, chapter 7, section 10].

It is safe to say that no one in this highly dysfunctional family was even attempting to achieve the IDEAL. When John exposed their ungodly and unlawful practices, it cost him his life. It is entirely probable, in light of Herod's sensitivity to criticism and his tendency to react harshly toward his critics, that the Pharisees who approached

Jesus that day in Perea were hoping to lure Jesus into making some public statement against the lifestyle of Herod. Knowing how this would infuriate him, it could potentially lead to the downfall, possibly even the death, of this troublemaker named Jesus. If not His destruction, then perhaps His public humiliation before one or more elements of Jewish society would suffice to remove Him as a threat. It would not be difficult to imagine such thoughts running through the minds of those who put their questions to Jesus in the tetrarchy of Herod Antipas.

As additional background information to the Matthew 19 account, it should be noted that during the time of Christ Jesus a heated debate was being waged among the Jews as to what constituted acceptable grounds for divorce. This also would assuredly be on the minds of the legalistic Pharisees when they asked, "Is it lawful for a man to divorce his wife for any and every reason?" [Matthew 19:3].

There were two main schools of thought on this controversial issue; an issue over which the Jews were very much divided. The Pharisees were undoubtedly confident that no matter how Jesus answered the question He was sure to incur the wrath of the followers of at least one of these theological positions. By involving Jesus in a very sensitive issue, both religiously and politically, He would surely be adversely affected in one way or another. The nature of the Lord's answer probably mattered little to these religionists; *any* response would certainly be sufficient to incite some faction of the Jewish population, and thus significantly reduce the popularity and effectiveness of Jesus. And, if His response resulted in the displeasure of Herod Antipas, all the better!

The school of Hillel and the school of Shammai were representative of the two major positions of the Jewish people with respect to the issue of what constituted "just cause" for a divorce. Both schools of thought permitted divorce. The disagreement was not over whether the dissolution of a covenant of marriage was permissible, but upon what basis it was permissible.

Rabbi Hillel's school of thought was very liberal and progressive. Divorce was allowed for almost every conceivable cause. Their reasoning was based upon their interpretation of the statement in the Law of Moses, "If a man marries a woman who becomes displeasing to him…" [Deuteronomy 24:1]. It was their understanding that "displeasing" was non-specific enough to permit the issuing of a certificate of divorce for virtually *any* cause. Indeed, Josephus, in *Antiquities of the Jews*, stated that a man may "be divorced from his wife for any cause whatsoever" [book 4, chapter 8, section 23]. Josephus, who lived during the majority of the first century A.D., was expressing the popular view of many during the time of Christ. He himself had been married three times, and divorced his second wife, by whom he had fathered three children, "not being pleased with her manners" [*The Life of Flavius Josephus*, sections 75-76]. The venerated Rabbi Akiba stated, "If any man saw a woman handsomer than his own wife, he might put his wife away; because it is said in the Law, 'If she find not favor in his eyes.'" Under this liberal theology, even burning the husband's bread could be cited as justifiable cause for the termination of the marital relationship.

On the other side of the heated debate stood the more conservative school of Shammai. Rabbi Shammai was far less flexible and lenient in his interpretation of Deuteronomy 24:1. It was his understanding of this passage from the Law that divorce was permissible only on the basis of sexual infidelity. When a husband, for example, found "some indecency" within his wife, this clearly signified sexual misconduct by the wife which violated her marital covenant. This, and this alone, was regarded as just cause for divorce by the school of Shammai.

With the philosophy of the school of Hillel so popular among the population, it is not surprising that the frequency of divorce during the time of Christ had reached scandalous proportions. Abuse of covenant partners abounded, the IDEAL was abandoned, and the sacred covenant of marriage was cheapened and tarnished by the deplorable behavior of God's people. Although a few remained faithful to their God and sought to uphold His IDEAL, such as the Qumran community which rejected the practice of divorce on *any* basis, they were noticeably in the minority.

Such, then, was the social, theological and political climate which provided the backdrop for the question of the Pharisees to Jesus in Matthew 19:3.

Jesus, much to their consternation, chose to respond to their question in a most unexpected manner. He determined to side with neither faction in the debate raging about Him, nor did He specifically speak out against the excesses of Herod. Instead, He chose a positive approach to the issue — He directed their minds back to God's IDEAL: "'Haven't you read,' He replied, 'that at the beginning the Creator "made them male and female," and said, "For this reason a man will leave his father and mother and be united to his wife, and the two will become one flesh"? So they are no longer two, but one. Therefore what God has joined together, let man not separate'" [Matthew 19:4-6]. The prophet Malachi employed much the same strategy. Before declaring God's hatred of divorce [Malachi 2:16], he sought to impress upon his people the fact that the Creator formed them all, and when they dealt treacherously with another of God's creatures they profaned a sacred trust [vs. 10].

By directing the minds of the Pharisees back to the original intent of the Creator, Jesus successfully side-stepped their plot to entrap Him. God's divine design called for the creation of both male and female, the latter being created specially for the former. It was the desire of the Creator for these two to join themselves together so closely and intimately they could, in a sense, become "one flesh." A separation of this union was never the intent of God.

Rather than siding with either faction, both of which allowed divorce, Jesus declared that if men were truly seeking God's IDEAL there would be no divorce at all. A failed marriage was an indication that at least one of the parties had chosen not to honor their vows, or to place the will of God above that of their own. When both spouses place the other above themselves, and commit themselves before God to achieve His IDEAL for their lives, the concept of divorce will never become a part of their thinking. Divorce can only enter a home when sin opens the door for it.

It should be noted that Jesus was not declaring the impossibility of a severed marital union. The Lord understood only too well the painful reality of divorce; it was rampant during His time. Jesus did not declare, "What God has joined together, man *cannot* separate." Although some insist that God will not recognize any divorce, or only those caused by the sexual immorality of one of the spouses, this is far more limiting than either reality or sound exegesis warrant. Jesus does not declare the impossibility of divorce; He declares it to be in opposition to the original intent of the Creator. It falls short of the IDEAL; it misses the mark. It is a failure which men and women committed to God and to one another should seek to avoid at all cost.

In essence, by restating God's IDEAL for marriage, Jesus sought to forever remove any justification for doing anything less than measuring up to God's expectations. The Jews were quibbling over what constituted "just cause" for a failure to achieve the IDEAL, and sought to involve Jesus by luring Him into the debate. Instead, Jesus made it abundantly clear that from the perspective of the throne of God, there is no such thing as justification for failing to achieve God's IDEAL.

Is this to suggest that both spouses involved in a divorce must stand equally condemned before God? Was Jesus refusing to acknowledge the existence of innocent victims? Not at all! Much of the teaching of God's Son with respect to this subject involves the determination of who must bear the responsibility, and thus the guilt and consequences, of a marital breakdown. Up to this point in the Lord's response to the Pharisees, however, He merely sought to impress upon the minds of an obstinate people obsessed with discovering legal loopholes that might permit or justify their treacherous behavior toward one another, that they were failing to consider their Creator's original design for marriage. Had their focus been different and their hearts more in tune with God, they would have been discussing ways to strengthen their marriages, rather than ways to terminate them. It was never God's desire to see those who were joined together in a covenant of marriage separate from one another. Neither should it be the desire of any of His creation.

"Why then did Moses command that a man give his wife a certificate of divorce and send her away?," asked the Pharisees [Matthew 19:7]. Once again, these religious leaders, blinded by their legalistic mindset, had completely missed the point. "Command" was probably much too strong, and even misleading, a word to utilize with reference to the provisions of law graciously provided by a God concerned over the affliction and suffering of an element of His people. Due to the sinful passions of selfish, self-willed mates, covenants of marriage were being dishonored and destroyed. Due to the hardness of their hearts toward both God and their spouses, God permitted the "putting away" of a spouse. This permissive law was in no way a reflection of God's approval of either the act or state of divorce, but primarily a protective measure: protecting an innocent husband from a faithless wife, and an innocent wife from a faithless husband. It was a law which served the victim, not the victimizer. It is vital to make a clear distinction between God's absolute will for mankind, His IDEAL, and the often necessary provisions He graciously enacts to limit the tragic effects of man's refusal to live according to the former. Laws which provide protection and relief for victims, and even legal separation from the one afflicting them, do not thereby condone the person or practices which made such laws necessary. Such unwarranted assumptions can quickly lead to a confused theology.

Jesus attempted to convey this truth to the Pharisees: "Moses permitted you to divorce your wives because your hearts were hard. But it was not this way from the beginning" [vs. 8]. Once again, the Lord attempted to direct their minds back to the IDEAL of their Creator. The minds of His questioners had become so clouded by a worldly perspective, and the countless tedious tenets of their religious system, that the beauty and simplicity of spiritual relationships ordered after the IDEAL evaded them. These legalistic religionists were not in need of a Messiah who would reduce the many popular justifications for divorce to a limited few, nor were they in need of a Messiah who would take the one "just cause" of the school of Shammai and expand it to many. They were in need of a Messiah who, like Jesus, refused to discuss cause, but instead held before them the beauty of the Creator's original design. The people of God were not in need of *legal* advice, they needed *spiritual* advice!

It was at this point in the discussion, and within this context, that

Jesus made His statement on divorce and remarriage, which will be examined in greater depth in the next chapter: "I tell you that anyone who divorces his wife, except for marital unfaithfulness, and marries another woman commits adultery" [vs. 9]. It should be noted that a few versions of the Bible (the *King James Version* and *American Standard Version*, for example) add the phrase: "And whoso marrieth her which is put away doth commit adultery."

There is very little evidence to warrant the inclusion of this phrase as part of the original text. Most likely it constitutes an expansion made by copyists seeking to accommodate this passage to Matthew 5:32. This certainly in no way is an effort to negate the truth reflected in this phrase, as some charge against the versions which omit it, since the same thought is acknowledged to be present in the Matthew 5:32 passage. If this were some devious plot on the part of modern translators to undermine truth, the phrase would have been deleted from the earlier passage as well. Instead, utilizing the art and science of textual criticism, translators have sought, through the correction of obvious errors which have crept into the text over the centuries, to provide as faithful a reproduction of the original text as humanly possible.

The Law of Moses, to which the Pharisees appealed in their discussion with Jesus that day in the tetrarchy of Herod Antipas, was far more a witness to the sinfulness of men's hearts than a revelation of God's intent for marriage. To perceive the heart of God, one would need to return to the beginning, not to the Law. This was what Jesus did. To facilitate and promote understanding of the will of God on this matter, one must perceive how it was "from the beginning," rather than seeking that insight from the legal provisions enacted due to the sinful attitudes and actions of men's hearts.

The disciples of Christ, as they reflected upon God's IDEAL for the marriage relationship, began to understand that one's covenant with one's mate was indeed a very serious commitment, one requiring a lifetime of devotion, patience and sacrifice to maintain. Some apparently began to wonder if the IDEAL was even humanly attainable. "The disciples said to Him, 'If this is the situation between a husband and wife, it is better not to marry"' [Matthew 19:10].

The disciples revealed by their statement they were still struggling with the influence of the current Jewish mindset. Commitment to a spouse was only for as long as it was felt to be convenient or pleasurable. Why go through all the strain and sacrifice of maintaining and maturing a relationship with one's spouse when it was so easy to simply terminate a floundering marriage and enter into a new one? The concept that marriage was a covenant that one was expected to honor for life was more than many of the Jewish men could fathom. "If I have to be tied down to just one woman for life, and work through every problem, and be patient with her flaws, then I might as well not get married at all" was an attitude infesting the minds of the people.

The fact that God's IDEAL was so shocking to these disciples demonstrated just how far mankind had drifted away from it. By showing them what God's original intent for marriage had been, Jesus challenged them to deeper spiritual reflection and renewed commitment to their interpersonal relationships. The time had come to turn away from a self-serving lifestyle, and to begin living spiritually mature lives before God. And what better place for this transformation of attitude and action to begin than in the home?!

The Gospel of Mark

In Mark 10:1-12 one will find the parallel to the Matthew 19 account. Although there are a great many similarities between these two versions of this incident in the life of Jesus, there are also some notable differences. For example, Mark records that the Pharisees asked Jesus, "Is it lawful for a man to divorce his wife?" The phrase "for any cause at all," which was included in Matthew's narrative, is absent from Mark's. This would appear to significantly alter the nature of the question being posed to Jesus. Rather than seeking to determine what causes for a divorce could be considered justifiable in the sight of God, the deletion implies the questioners were perhaps seeking to determine if the state of divorce itself was justifiable.

The response of Jesus, in the text of Mark's chronicle, essentially declares: Divorce was reluctantly permitted by God, but He regarded it as an abhorrent alternative to the IDEAL. Further, it was only permitted due to the hardness of their hearts, not because it ever constituted a part of the Creator's original plan. God's design was that these covenant relationships *not* be terminated; they were created to endure. Sinful, willful men, however, had different ideas, and they began breaking their covenants and putting away their wives for some of the most frivolous causes. The fact that a merciful God issued various laws to help alleviate the negative effects upon the victims of these self-willed acts, in no way suggested His approval of those acts. Jesus acknowledged that God did indeed *permit* divorce, but He hastened to clarify that God did not thereby *approve* of it.

One will also notice in Mark's rendition of this event that the persons who uttered the words "command" and "permit" are reversed from Matthew's account. In Matthew, the Pharisees asked, "Why then did Moses command that a man give his wife a certificate of divorce and send her away?," to which Jesus replied, "Moses permitted you to divorce your wives because your hearts were hard." In Mark, however, one discovers Jesus asking the Pharisees, in response to their question as to the lawfulness of divorce, "What did Moses command you?" In reply, the Pharisees said, "Moses permitted a man to write a certificate of divorce and send her away." Jesus then clarified this by saying, "It was because your hearts were hard that Moses wrote you this law."

A possible explanation for this reversal of word usage is that Matthew and Mark may well have been focusing in upon different aspects of the discussion that evolved that day. Early on in the exchange, the Pharisees perhaps were more intent upon the issue of what constituted justifiable cause for a divorce, and in the course of their conversation utilized the word "command." This was the topic upon which Matthew reported in his Gospel record.

As the discussion evolved, the Pharisees may have shifted their focus somewhat and inquired as to the lawfulness of the state of divorce itself, a line of inquiry preserved in the Gospel of Mark. Perhaps testing their understanding of what He had stated earlier in the conversation, Jesus might have used their own expression "command" in His question, to which they correctly responded that this was merely "permitted."

It is suggested by some scholars that one can detect a progression of thought in the exchange of the Pharisees with Jesus. If that was indeed the case, and it is at least a logical premise, then the deletion of a specific phrase and the reversal of the users of specific words, can be reasonably reconciled.

The apparent evolution of thought, or progression in the nature and focus of the discussion, may also shed some light on another difference between the Matthew and Mark accounts of this incident. In Matthew's record one finds the phrase, "except for marital unfaithfulness," which is generally referred to as the "exception clause," whereas Mark makes no mention of it. Perhaps it should also be noted here that neither Luke, Paul, nor any other inspired writer indicates any awareness of this statement by Jesus. It appears *only* in Matthew. If indeed, as has been suggested, Matthew was more focused on the issue of cause, the inclusion in his account of a clause dealing with that specific topic is understandable; nor is it surprising to find it excluded from those accounts which have a somewhat different emphasis.

A final major difference between the records of Matthew and Mark is that in the latter Jesus mentions the possibility of a woman initiating a divorce against her husband. "Anyone who divorces his wife and marries another woman commits adultery against her. And if she divorces her husband and marries another man, she commits adultery" [Mark 10:11-12]. Jesus was not advocating a woman's right to now begin doing unto husbands what husbands had previously been doing unto them. Traditionally, a woman had been unable to initiate a divorce; that was regarded as the man's right. Times were changing, however. Women were beginning to assert themselves, sometimes positively, sometimes negatively. Jesus was aware of these changes; He knew of Salome's situation, for example; and He addressed His remarks on divorce and remarriage to *both* sexes.

The Gospel of Luke

In Luke's Gospel record one finds a very brief statement concerning divorce and remarriage sandwiched between the parables of the Unrighteous Steward and the Rich Man and Lazarus. "Anyone who divorces his wife and marries another woman commits adultery, and the man who marries a divorced woman commits adultery" [Luke 16:18].

Once again, Jesus is found speaking to the Pharisees [vs. 14], a religious group whose hearts had become exceedingly worldly and callous. For the sake of their own traditions, they increasingly minimized the laws of God. As they drew farther away from God, they sought desperately to find ways to portray their behavior as justified before God and men. "You are the ones who justify yourselves in the eyes of men, but God knows your hearts. What is highly valued among men is detestable in God's sight" [vs. 15].

It is very probable, from the surrounding context, that Jesus briefly referred to the issue of divorce and remarriage at this time as an illustration of the devious devices of the Pharisees. Their views and practices in this area were far removed from the IDEAL, nevertheless they sought to justify their deviation from the original intent of the Creator. Although their practices and preferences were "highly valued among men," God found them detestable. In a very strongly worded statement, Jesus denounced their feeble attempts to justify their numerous abuses of their covenants of marriage.

The Gospel of John

Although the Gospel of John contains no direct teaching on the subject of divorce and remarriage, there is one passage in the fourth chapter that should probably not be overlooked in any discussion of this topic.

Jesus and His disciples were traveling from Judea to Galilee and had stopped briefly to rest at Jacob's well in the city of Sychar. Leaving Jesus alone at the well, the disciples went into town to purchase food. While He was resting, a Samaritan woman came to the well to draw water, whereupon Jesus asked her for a drink. This greatly surprised the woman, for Jews and Samaritans had been feuding with one another for generations. "How is it that You, being a Jew, ask me for a drink since I am a Samaritan woman?" [vs. 9].

Jesus informed her that if she only knew who He was, she would be asking Him for living water; water which would cause the one who drank it never to thirst again; "a spring of water welling up to eternal life" [vs. 13-14]. The woman replied, "Sir, give me this water so that I won't get thirsty and have to keep coming here to draw water" [vs. 15].

At this point in the conversation an exchange occurred between Jesus and the Samaritan woman which a few scholars feel may have some bearing on the issue of divorce and remarriage. Jesus instructed the woman, "Go, call your husband and come back."

"I have no husband," she replied. Then Jesus said to her, "You are right when you say you have no husband. The fact is, you have had five husbands, and the man you now have is not your husband. What you have just said is quite true" [vs. 16-18].

There has been considerable deliberation and debate as to exactly what the Lord sought to convey in this statement about the Samaritan woman's prior and present relationships. Some have theorized that the woman may have been a prostitute, having "had" (in the sexual sense) five married men as paying partners, and was now offering her services to a sixth. Jesus, thus, correctly stated she had no husband of her own, but instead had "had sexually" several men who were husbands (i.e.: who were married men).

Other scholars are convinced the woman had actually been married five times, and that each of those marriages had come to an end. Whether they had been dissolved by divorce, or by death, or a combination of the two, is not specified. Although some have criticized this view by stating the number of relationships is unrealistic, such behavior is not altogether uncommon, either then or now. The Sadducees, on one occasion, questioned Jesus about the fate of a woman, following the resurrection, who had been married to seven men, all of whom had preceded her in death [Matthew 22:23-28]. It is not inconceivable, therefore, that the Samaritan woman had outlived five husbands. Nor is it inconceivable that some or all of those marriages may have been terminated by divorce. There is simply no basis whatsoever for choosing one over the other. Either is a reasonable deduction.

The fact that Jesus stated she was now with a man who was not her husband has led some to question her moral character, and to assume her previous relationships were therefore less than honorable. If indeed her present relationship was a sinful one, this would certainly not reflect well upon her character. It could indeed lead one to assume her prior marriages had ended because her husbands found within her "some indecency."

These views are all speculative, however; there is simply not sufficient information supplied in the text to determine with any degree of certainty the nature of this woman's character or relationships. By examining her in the worst possible light one might claim she was either a prostitute or an immoral woman with whom no husband could long endure. In the best possible light, one could surmise she had simply been widowed five times and was now in a relationship with a man with whom she had not yet entered into a covenant of marriage. Either view is logical and consistent with the facts as presented in the account. Further complicating the matter, Jesus neither condemns nor condones her past; He merely indicates His awareness of it.

To attempt to formulate any kind of theology concerning divorce and remarriage from this passage, as some have tried, is completely unwarranted by all principles of sound exegesis. Thus, the account is mentioned in passing in this study, but will not be further consulted in the examination of the teaching of Jesus Christ.

These few Scriptures from the Gospel records constitute the entirety of the Lord's teaching on the subject of divorce and remarriage. Although He may well have said more about it to His disciples, these few words are all that God chose to preserve for us. Any theology which claims to be founded upon the teaching of Jesus Christ will have to be formulated from these few comments alone.

Chapter 6
The Teaching of Jesus Christ

Having noted the various passages in the gospel records which deal with the topic of divorce and remarriage, and having placed them in their historical, cultural and theological context, one must now seek to understand the message the Lord sought to convey in those limited number of references. Rather than again examining each Scripture separately, the focus will instead be upon each of the key elements of the teaching Jesus proclaimed. By comprehending each individually, in a logical sequence, one can perhaps come to better appreciate and perceive the entirety of His instruction on this subject.

THE REALITY OF DIVORCE & REMARRIAGE

Despite one's feelings about the issue of divorce and remarriage, there is simply no denying the fact that Jesus acknowledges the reality of failed marriages and the subsequent formation of new marital relationships. Although contrary to the spirit of God's original design, covenants of marriage *can* be broken and dissolved. Throughout the references in the gospel records, Jesus repeatedly spoke of a spouse "divorcing" his or her mate, and of both subsequently entering into a state of "marriage" with another.

One should not overlook the significance of the words and phrases Jesus chose to use, and chose not to use, in characterizing these two states. Each term utilized clearly denotes the severing of a relationship. These divorces were *not* merely temporary separations or marriages on hold, with the covenant itself remaining in force. They are characterized as nothing less than a total dissolution of a marriage. Those who had previously been united as one, were now two again. The "one flesh" state had been terminated.

Some within the religious world deny that *any* divorce is ever recognized by God. They maintain that it is an absolute impossibility to sever that which God has joined together as one. Once married, always married, 'till death do you part! Although it is acknowledged by those who maintain this view that a certificate of divorce may indeed be acquired, and the couple may live apart from one another, nevertheless the covenant of marriage itself, in the eyes of God, has *not* been rescinded. The cancellation of the covenant of marriage, it is claimed, is only effected by the death of one or both of the partners to it.

By embracing this position one is then bound to accept the next logical conclusion arising from out of it: any subsequent union of either spouse is not actually a "marriage," but rather an "adulterous affair." The state of remarriage, therefore, becomes a state of "living in sin." No other conclusion can rationally be maintained if one accepts the original premise that only death can terminate a covenant of marriage.

Although this teaching is not uncommon in the religious world today, a careful study of the Scriptures, and especially of the teaching of Jesus Christ, will quickly reveal that it has no validity. The Lord never once characterized a second union of a divorced man or woman as "living in sin." Indeed, this phrase is *nowhere* utilized in Scripture with reference to this subject; it is the invention of men, not the instruction of Christ.

The term Jesus used to refer to a second union of a divorced man or woman was "marriage."

"I tell you that anyone who divorces his wife … and *marries* another woman …" [Matthew 19:9]. "Anyone who divorces his wife and *marries* another woman … And if she divorces her husband and *marries* another man…" [Mark 10:11-12]. "Anyone who divorces his wife and *marries* another woman" [Luke 16:18]. Those who claim that a second union is not a marriage, claim far more than Jesus did! Further, those who refuse to acknowledge the reality of a divorce, also deny far more than Jesus did.

Such statements as, "Christians should regard no one as being really divorced," and "Those who are divorced thereby become unfit for any further association ... they can never again enter into a covenant of marriage," both of which were recently declared publicly by religious leaders, reflect a theology formulated from a source other than the teaching of Jesus Christ.

Generally, those who promote such a stern theology cite the following statement of the Lord as "proof" of their position: "'For this reason a man will leave his father and mother and be united to his wife, and the two will become one flesh.' So they are no longer two, but one. Therefore what God has joined together, let man not separate" [Matthew 19:5-6; Mark 10:7-9]. The last word in this passage is "chorizo" (see chapter four), which means "to sever, disunite, put asunder, separate, divide." Few would question the fact that it denotes a total division, a rending apart, of that which was previously united. The disunity which Jesus disparages in this statement is that of a marriage covenant. It was never a part of God's original design, His IDEAL, that such unions be severed. However, this in no way suggests that such severing is beyond the scope of possibility. The Lord is not stating man *cannot* separate this sacred union, rather He insists men *ought* not do so, for it violates the spirit and intent of God's design for marriage. To insist, as do some, that a marriage is not truly severed because the Lord has prohibited such dissolutions, is little different than claiming a dead man has not truly been severed from life, or the realm of the living, since God has prohibited murder. The prohibition declares the act unacceptable, and even sinful, but it does not render it impossible or unachievable, nor does it negate the inevitable consequences which result.

When Jesus used the phrase, "let man not separate," the Greek verb for "separate" appears in the present imperative form, and is preceded by the negative particle "me," which makes this a "prohibitive imperative" in Greek grammatical construction. Simply stated, this signifies a negative command which serves the purpose of prohibiting the continuance of a specific act already taking place. This phrase could just as correctly be translated, "Therefore what God has joined together, *stop* separating." Maintaining that one *cannot* separate that which was previously joined together fails to perceive the significance of this Greek phrase. Marriages were being terminated. Jesus acknowledged that reality. His command to them was, "STOP!" The intent was to forbid the continuance of what was, not to declare the impossibility of it.

Covenants of marriage were being broken; new marriages were being entered into; and all was being done with little regard for God's IDEAL, or for the hurt being inflicted upon others. This was a reality of which Jesus was painfully aware. Thus, He called them to cease their sinful behavior and refocus their hearts upon God's original design for marriage. It was a call to reassessment and repentance; a call to recapture the beauty of God's IDEAL, and to forever put behind them this frivolous fracturing of relationships.

EXAMINING THE EXCEPTION CLAUSE

In order to fully comprehend the teaching of Jesus Christ with regard to divorce and remarriage, it is imperative that the true significance of the so-called "exception clause," which is found only in Matthew's gospel record, be determined. "But I tell you that anyone who divorces his wife, except for marital unfaithfulness, causes her to become an adulteress, and anyone who marries the divorced woman commits adultery" [Matthew 5:32]. "I tell you that anyone who divorces his wife, except for marital unfaithfulness, and marries another woman commits adultery" [Matthew 19:9].

There have been numerous theories proffered as to the interpretation of this somewhat puzzling clause. To make the task even more challenging, there has been considerable debate over the exact meaning of a particular Greek word in the clause and how it should be translated.

The highly contested Greek word, which is variously translated, is "porneia." Some translations render this phrase "except for fornication" or "except for immorality." Others have "sexual sin," "marital unfaithfulness," "lewd conduct," "unchastity," and other similar expressions. An examination of the first four letters of this word (as transliterated into English) — PORN — will suggest to the reader some of the words in our vocabulary which are derived from it (such as pornography).

A good, general, operational definition of this word is "any illicit sexual activity." As one can quickly perceive, this is broad enough to embrace a wide variety of such illicit activity, including incest, prostitution, homosexuality, child molestation, and bestiality, just to name a few. It is also general enough in scope to encompass all illicit sexual activity engaged in both prior to and following a covenant of marriage. There is nothing inherent within the word itself that suggests this activity is restricted solely to the premarital state, although some promote such a view. It should also not be overlooked that "porneia" is used in the New Testament writings to discuss acts of lewdness, uncleanness, and even idolatry. Thus, one can easily see the word has a very wide range of meaning and application.

Some scholars, embracing the view that "porneia" refers exclusively to illicit sexual activity *prior* to a covenant of marriage, maintain Jesus teaches in the exception clause that the *only* acceptable cause of divorce is the discovery by one of the spouses, *after* a covenant of marriage has been effected, that their mate had committed some illicit sexual act *prior* to their covenant of marriage. If a man believed his wife to have been a virgin at the time of their marriage, for example, only to discover later that she had been sexually active prior to their relationship, then, according to this view, he has "just cause" to terminate the covenant of marriage. To help validate this perception of the exception clause they cite Deuteronomy 22:13-21, and also the determination of Joseph to divorce Mary.

Other scholars view "porneia" as encompassing far more than just the *physical* aspects of an illicit sexual act; it is perceived as constituting any illicit *spiritual* activity as well. If one's spouse commits spiritual fornication with the world – if they are an idolater, or one who is engaged in a love affair with worldly pleasures, or simply an unbeliever, for example — this also is seen as "just cause" for divorce. In their opinion, this is the significance of Paul's statement to the saints in the city of Corinth: "But if the unbeliever leaves, let him do so. A believing man or woman is not bound in such circumstances" [1 Corinthians

7:15].

Since the meaning and usage of "porneia" is so broad, even within the pages of the New Testament writings, it is rather inappropriate for any person or group to declare dogmatically that Jesus had only *one* of these many conceivable applications in mind when He issued His so-called "exception clause." There is simply no obvious, indisputable basis upon which to make such a narrow determination. Since the Lord Himself chose not to specify any particular application or meaning, it is at least logical to assume He may have intended it to be far more general than specific. After all, any of the many aspects of "*porneia*" would be sufficient in and of itself to seriously jeopardize a covenant of marriage, if not destroy it. Why single out only one when each represents such a real threat to this sacred union?

Tremendous debate and division has been generated in the religious world over these two views, and many tend to rally around one or the other, or versions thereof. However, there is another interpretation that bears careful consideration, and which may well come closer to capturing the intent of Christ Jesus. It is just possible the Lord was not giving an acceptable exception at all. The notion that Jesus was admitting to a *single* "just cause" for failing to achieve God's IDEAL may well be a false premise upon which numerous false doctrines have been constructed.

The man-made term "exception clause" is a very misleading one; *nowhere* is it so characterized in Scripture. If one carefully considers the teaching of Jesus on this issue throughout the gospel records, one will note Jesus repeatedly refused to acquiesce to the popular and prevailing views of His day, each of which acknowledged various "just causes" for divorce. Some schools of thought insisted that there was only one just cause for terminating a covenant of marriage; other schools maintained "any and every cause" was justified. Jesus held high for observation the IDEAL, and refused to acknowledge *any* justifiable cause for failure to achieve it. Yes, Jesus was aware that marriages were failing; He was aware that there were a great many reasons for these failures; but to justify any or all of them, as men were attempting to do, would be to diminish the majesty of God's IDEAL for marriage.

If it is true that Jesus was in fact offering *no* exceptions to the Creator's original design for marital relationships — one man for one woman for life — what is one to make of this apparent "exception clause" recorded in Matthew's gospel? There are two possible explanations. The first is that this clause may be an example of a "preterition," which means the exception of which Jesus speaks is an exception to the proposition of the text itself, rather than to a specific verb within the proposition. Thus, the passage might well be translated: "Anyone who divorces his wife — the permission of Moses in Deuteronomy 24:1f notwithstanding — and marries another woman commits adultery." This effectively removes any exception to the IDEAL concept, and makes the intent of the message far more consistent with other statements of the Lord within the context: "The Law says ... but I say ...!" Jesus would thus be issuing a New Dispensation challenge to the people of God: although the Law of Moses permitted certain acts due to the hardness of their hearts, it was *not* so from the beginning; it was never a part of the Creator's divine design. Under the New Covenant, mankind is called to return to the IDEAL; to begin living on a vastly superior spiritual plane; to begin behaving as the children of God. Permission to do otherwise is no longer granted. The permissive provisions of law, due to hardness of heart, are now terminated.

A second probable interpretation, and one very much compatible with the first, is that this so-called exception clause is simply a means whereby responsibility or guilt for the breakdown of the covenant of marriage is ascribed to one spouse or the other. If a man puts away his wife, and she has done absolutely nothing to warrant such an action on his part, *he* is the one who must bear the responsibility for the dissolution of the marriage. However, if the wife is guilty of "*porneia*" then *she* must bear the guilt for the ultimate breakdown of the relationship, even though it may have been her husband who actually sought and secured the certificate of divorce against her.

Thus, the Lord's "*exception* clause" is in reality no such thing; Jesus was merely assigning responsibility for the ultimate destruction of the marital relationship. If the husband was dealing treacherously with his wife, *he* must bear the guilt; if the wife was not behaving according to the vows of her covenant, *she* must bear the guilt. In either case a marriage has ended, but the matter of culpability has now been addressed. This view also has the advantage of being much easier to reconcile with the remainder of Scripture, in which no mention is ever made of any such "exception."

Perhaps one explanation for why the religious world has so woefully misunderstood this teaching of the Lord is that the focus of God's people has been misdirected. While Jesus lifts up the Creator's original design for marriage — the IDEAL — men squander their time and energy searching for some legal justification for their failure to embrace it. With seared consciences and hardened hearts men seek ways to "legally" circumvent their responsibility to both God and their spouses. Divorce is a concept foreign to the heart focused upon God and His IDEAL; it is a worldly option sought out and embraced only by one whose focus is inward, and whose god is SELF. Jesus refused to dignify such maneuvering by declaring any aspect of it "just."

Do marriages end? Yes, and with a frequency that grieves the Lord. Divorce is a tragic reality of life, of which the Lord is painfully aware, but it is not the will of God that marriages end, rather it is the will of man. When divorces occur people get hurt; sometimes innocent people, through no fault of their own. In such cases, one spouse must bear the responsibility for this destroyed covenant of marriage, and also the guilt. It is the assigning of this responsibility and culpability which Jesus addresses in the so-called "*exception* clause" of Matthew's gospel record; a fact which will become increasingly clear as His teaching on this subject is examined in greater depth.

THE MEANING OF "ADULTERY"

The one term which seems to generate the most difficulty in the minds of biblical students, and the most debate and division among biblical scholars, is "adultery." The way in which this word is translated, interpreted, and applied has proved to be a most sensitive issue. What exactly was the intent of Jesus when He stated on several occasions that when a divorce and/or remarriage occurs, one or more of the parties "committed adultery?"

Particularly relevant to a correct understanding of the Lord's teaching with regard to this issue is the proper identification of the verb forms utilized. Indeed, this will prove to be a major factor at this point in clarifying the teaching of Jesus. A failure to distinguish, and correctly identify and translate, these forms will lead to doctrines greatly at odds with the original intent of the Lord. One simply cannot stress strongly enough how critical these verb forms are to correct interpretation.

In the recorded words of Jesus Christ, with reference to divorce and remarriage, three different groups of people are being examined: (1) the one who divorces a spouse, (2) the spouse who has been put away, and (3) the person who later marries one who has been divorced. In each of these three situations, adultery is said to occur. Also, Jesus speaks to each of these three groups about the matter of responsibility and guilt for the divorce, who must bear it, and the nature of the subsequent consequences. Prior to examining what Jesus has to say to each of these groups, however, one must first seek to grasp the biblical concept of adultery.

The definition most commonly found in the various English language dictionaries on the market is: "Sexual intercourse between a married person and someone other than their spouse." As a result of this popular and widely accepted definition, most people, when they hear the word adultery, conjure up the image of a married man or woman cheating on their spouse by having sex with another partner.

There is no question but what this popular definition of the word was utilized by the biblical writers as well. Such a view of adultery is seen in several places. In John 8:3-11 one discovers the account of a woman, brought before Jesus in the temple courts, who had been caught in the very act of adultery. There is little doubt that the act being referred to was sexual in nature. Hebrews 13:4 is another passage where sexual misconduct is obviously in view: "Marriage should be honored by all, and the marriage bed kept pure, for God will judge the adulterer and all the sexually immoral." Within the pages of the Old Testament writings, the prophet Ezekiel draws a very vivid picture of two adulterous sisters, describing in graphic detail their sexual misconduct [Ezekiel 23]. Thus, there is no question but what the biblical definition of adultery does indeed include the concept of sexual unfaithfulness of a married man or woman.

It simply must not be overlooked, however, that the above definition is far from being the *only* one presented in Scripture. The fact is, the Greek noun "moicheia," which is generally translated "adultery," has several other biblical meanings and usages. For example, it can refer to a sexual *attitude* separate and apart from the sexual *act* itself. "You have heard that it was said, 'Do not commit adultery.' But I tell you that anyone who looks at a woman lustfully has already committed adultery with her in his heart" [Matthew 5:28]. Is it possible to commit adultery without ever actually engaging in the physical aspects of the act itself? Can one "commit adultery" alone? Yes, according to the teaching of Jesus. It is possible for adultery to occur entirely and exclusively within the heart and mind of the lusting individual. Thus, adultery can be as much an *attitude* as an *act*.

Within the *Haggadic* sections of the *Talmud* and *Midrash* one will find numerous warnings against adultery, and it is frequently characterized as being far more than a mere physical sexual act. "We find that even he who commits adultery with the eyes is called an adulterer," and a reference to Job 24:15 follows. "He who regards a woman with lustful intention is as one who cohabits with her."

"He who touches the little finger of a woman is as one who touches a certain spot." Thus, from a realistic point of view, adultery does not merely consist of physical intercourse with one who is not one's spouse; adultery is present already in the very desire of the heart.

"Moicheia" is also used within the pages of the sacred writings to convey a condition of unfaithfulness to God; a breach of one's covenant relationship with one's Creator. One noted Greek scholar observes that Hebraistically and figuratively this particular word is equivalent to: Faithless to God, unclean, apostate, ungodly. Some suggest the focus is even narrower in the New Testament dispensation: it constitutes being "unfaithful to God" by virtue of one's "rejection of Jesus."

Christ Jesus more than once referred to the people of His day as "a wicked and adulterous generation" because of their lack of faith [Matthew 12:39; 16:4], or because they were ashamed of the Lord and His teachings [Mark 8:38], and were thus unwilling to follow Him obediently.

Therefore, according to the Scriptures, adultery can be regarded figuratively as a breach of covenant with one's Lord; a breach which can be effected by any number of sinful, rebellious acts. In this sense, adultery is viewed as being far more than the performance of specific acts, but rather the breach of covenant itself which was generated by those acts. When Jesus spoke of His fellow countrymen as being "adulterers" and an "adulterous generation," He was commenting upon far more than their specific sins; He was focusing upon the resultant state of separation of this people from their Creator produced by those sinful acts. It was just as the prophet stated centuries earlier, "Your iniquities have separated you from your God" [Isaiah 59:2].

"Moicheia" is further utilized repeatedly in the Bible to characterize those who are worldly and unspiritual in their actions and attitudes. The brother of Jesus, after describing individuals who were quarreling among themselves over various selfish worldly desires, wrote, "You adulterous people, don't you know that friendship with the world is hatred toward God?" [James 4:4]. The apostle Peter spoke of false, corrupt teachers as being little better than brute beasts who "revel in their pleasures," who are always sinning against God, and who, "with eyes full of adultery," seduce away the unsuspecting after their falsehoods [2 Peter 2]. The self-proclaimed prophetess Jezebel was one such seductress who enticed some of the saints in Thyatira to "commit adultery with her" by engaging in worldly, immoral behavior, and through sacrifices offered to idols [Revelation 2:20-22].

As was seen with Jezebel and her disciples, it was not uncommon for "*moicheia*" to express itself in the form of idolatry; such is often labeled "adultery." Ezekiel 16 speaks of unfaithful Jerusalem as being like a prostitute, an adulteress, because of her repeated acts of idolatry. Even among the ancient Apostolic Fathers idolatry was recognized as constituting adultery. Referring to the practice of idol worship,

121

Clement wrote, "Whoever acts as the heathen do, commits adultery" [2 Clement 4:3]. In the *Shepherd of Hermas* (in his second work, known as *Commands*), one reads, "Now they commit adultery, not only who pollute their flesh, but who also make an image. If therefore a woman perseveres in any thing of this kind, and repents not, depart from her, and live not with her, otherwise thou also shalt be partaker of her sin" [4:9]. Some scholars detect a possible connection here with the statement of Paul to the Corinthians: "But if the unbeliever leaves, let him do so. A believing man or woman is not bound in such circumstances" [1 Corinthians 7:15]. According to the above definition, the unbeliever in this passage would be regarded as an adulterer; not because he had committed an illicit sexual act with one other than his spouse, but because he was in a loving relationship with the world rather than with God.

In the secular writings of that day and age, *"moicheia"* had an even broader range of possible meaning. Some applied it to sexual relationships between men and animals; others utilized it to denote the intermingling of people from different racial groups. Some even taught there was an astrological connection: that fornication and adultery were more likely to be engaged in when Venus was in conjunction with Mars. Although such secular views never found their way into the Scriptures, nevertheless the inspired writers and those who read their works may well have been aware of them.

It should be rather obvious, therefore, from this admittedly brief and incomplete overview, that adultery, as understood within the pages of the Scriptures, simply cannot be limited exclusively to the narrow definition of "an illicit sexual act between a married person and one other than their spouse."

As one carefully examines all the many facets of the biblical concept of adultery, one soon begins to realize that the concept itself has a greater focus and broader scope than any specific part of the whole. In other words, the concept of adultery, as presented in the pages of Scripture, appears to be more the resultant breakdown or breach of a covenant, than any specific act itself, of which there are many, which may have generated that effect. By limiting the meaning of *"moicheia"* to only *one* of its many biblical usages, and then maintaining that this *alone* is adultery, one will have great difficulty understanding the teaching of Jesus with respect to divorce and remarriage. However, if one regards *"moicheia"* as a resultant breakdown of a covenant relationship, for which there are numerous possible causes, one will appreciate far more the significance of the Lord's teaching, and one's practical theology will be more in tune with the will of God.

When Jesus declares that adultery has been committed, He is stating far more than the fact of two people engaging in a physical sex act. He is declaring the fact of a *broken covenant* between a husband and wife. Although sexual infidelity may well have ultimately been the cause of some of those disunions, there is little doubt that in some of the Lord's statements about divorce and remarriage sexual infidelity is not even remotely being alluded to when He utilizes the word adultery, as will soon be demonstrated.

It is divorce itself that Jesus focuses upon and condemns, far more so than any particular cause that may have generated that dissolution of marriage. There are countless causes for the failure of marriages, but it is the failure of marriage itself that Jesus says is unacceptable before God. *"Moicheia,"* therefore, refers to the actual *breach of the covenant*, the breakdown of the marriage relationship, for which there may be a host of causes. This is a view which can be clearly demonstrated from all the biblical passages in which this word appears. By allowing oneself to become side-tracked by the English dictionary's definition of adultery as being strictly a sexual act, one fails to perceive the true biblical meaning and application of this word, which is the idea of unfaithfulness to a covenant relationship; an unfaithfulness which may manifest itself in a number of ways.

The spouse who is guilty of "committing adultery," then, is the spouse responsible for violating his or her covenant of marriage and bringing about the destruction of this sacred relationship. The cause may well have been sexual misconduct, but it may also have been something else entirely. The adultery of which Jesus speaks is unfaithfulness to the covenant itself, and to the other party to that covenant, not a solitary, singular act which might have contributed to that breach. "Moicheia" is simply not as limited in scope as many interpreters seek to make it. To truly understand the teaching of Jesus, it is critical that one shift his focus from cause to effect.

JESUS ADDRESSES INDIVIDUAL SITUATIONS

As has already been mentioned, when teaching on the subject of divorce and remarriage, Jesus addressed Himself to three different groups of individuals and the unique situations they each faced. To some He had a message of rebuke; to others a message of hope and healing. By carefully examining the information imparted to each, one will begin to develop an awareness of the gracious teaching of the Lord with respect to this issue.

#1 — THE ONE WHO DIVORCES HIS/HER SPOUSE. "Anyone who divorces his wife, except for marital unfaithfulness, and marries another woman commits adultery" [Matthew 19:9]. "If she divorces her husband and marries another man, she commits adultery" [Mark 10:12]. "Anyone who divorces his wife and marries another woman commits adultery" [Luke 16:18].

The basic concern underlying each of these statements about the breakdown of a covenant of marriage is: who is responsible for this disunion? Who must bear the burden of guilt for this breach of covenant? If one spouse decides that they no longer wish to remain married to the other, and they seek out and secure a divorce, and then join themselves in marriage to another, it is *this* spouse who commits adultery/breaks covenant, *not* the put away spouse. The initiating spouse alone bears the responsibility and guilt for the severed marriage. An exception to this would be if the put away spouse had behaved in such a way as to violate the covenant, thus bringing about the divorce (as with faithless Israel and God, who was forced to divorce her). In such an event, the spouse who initiated the divorce would not bear the guilt for the breakdown; it would shift to the unfaithful spouse. This, again, clearly demonstrates the significance of the Lord's so-called exception clause.

CASE HISTORY — *Bill and Marcie have been joined in marriage for five years. In recent months, Bill has begun spending more and more time with his male companions. They go out every night, even spend weekends together. It becomes increasingly clear that Bill has little desire to spend time with Marcie, or work on developing their relationship. She becomes less and less significant to him; he's far more interested in worldly pursuits, and his "male bonding," than his marital responsibilities. One day he presents Marcie with a certificate of divorce. "Marriage is just too restrictive. I need my freedom," he explains. Two years later he meets Cathy, and they get married.*

One of the questions posed by the above example is: who was responsible for the breakdown of this marriage? Who must bear the guilt for failing to achieve God's IDEAL? Applying the words of Jesus to this situation, and assuming Marcie was not unfaithful to her vows, Bill must assume the guilt of committing adultery.

Some, viewing adultery only as an act of sexual infidelity, maintain Bill did not actually commit adultery until two years after the divorce when he married Cathy. Maintaining such a position, however, implies Jesus was not really condemning Bill's breaking his covenant of marriage with Marcie, but rather was condemning the "adulterous union" with Cathy two years later. Jesus, therefore, is portrayed as being far more concerned with the fact of a subsequent sexual union, than with the dissolution of a sacred covenant of marriage.

Such reasoning makes a mockery of the Lord's teaching! When one finally comes to understand that "moicheia" means far more than mere sexual misconduct, but rather the breach of covenant which can result from a host of causes, one will begin to understand more clearly the focus of Jesus and that which truly distresses Him in these tragic situations involving divorce and remarriage.

CASE HISTORY — *Tom and Debbie had been joined in marriage twelve years when Tom discovered his wife was having an affair with his best friend Jack. Unbeknownst to Tom, this had been*

125

going on for months. When confronted, Debbie acknowledged the infidelity. She stopped seeing Jack for a while, but eventually began the affair again. They went to marriage counseling, spoke to their church leaders, and various family members got involved, but all to no avail. Debbie refused to give up her sexual relationship with Jack. With a heavy heart, Tom sought out an attorney and secured a divorce against Debbie.

In the above situation, it was Tom who sought and secured a divorce against his wife, but who was actually responsible for the breakdown of this covenant of marriage? Was it Tom, since he was the one who presented Debbie with a certificate of divorce? Or, was it Debbie, since it was her immoral conduct which forced Tom to seek the solution he did? Who was the guilty party? Again, we see the significance of the Lord's *exception* clause. Although Tom divorced Debbie, it was the latter who must bear both the guilt and the responsibility for the destruction of the covenant of marriage.

Thus, to this first group of individuals to whom Jesus speaks in the gospel records, the Lord clearly states that the one who initiates a divorce against a spouse is the one who must bear the responsibility and guilt for that dissolution, *except* in a case where the divorce was sought due to the destructive and ungodly behavior of the spouse being put away. In such events, it is the put away spouse who must bear the burden of guilt and responsibility.

#2 — THE ONE WHO HAS BEEN PUT AWAY BY A SPOUSE.

"Anyone who divorces his wife, except for marital unfaithfulness, causes her to become an adulteress" [Matthew 5:32]. "Anyone who divorces his wife and marries another woman commits adultery against her" [Mark 10:11]. At first glance, these two passages seem to be declaring two separate and distinct truths. Closer examination, however, will reveal that both proclaim the very same message.

In Matthew's account, Jesus makes the observation that when a man divorces his wife he causes her to become an adulteress. The wording of most translations here conveys the concept that a man, simply by virtue of the act of divorcing his wife, even though she may be the "innocent party" in the situation, can thereby cause her to become an adulteress. One might well ask: in what possible sense does this divorced woman become an adulteress?!

The traditional response to this has always been that she, being subject to the desires of the flesh, will one day seek a relationship with another man. When that happens, and when they give in to their sexual passions, at that point she becomes guilty of adultery. This assumes her marriage to her husband is still in force (since God will not actually recognize any such divorce; after all, what God has joined together, man *cannot* separate), and that adultery is strictly limited to a sexual act. And God forbid that this woman and her male friend should ever marry; they would then be "living in adultery," with each and every subsequent act of sexual intimacy constituting an additional charge of adultery marked against them!

One does not have to be blessed with a great deal of insight or common sense to detect this view has a multitude of problems connected with it. What if the put away woman should choose *not* to seek a relationship with another, but instead lives the remainder of her life celibate? Examples of women, and men, doing just this abound. Is she still an adulteress? Jesus does not state, nor does He even imply, the husband causes his wife to be an adulteress *only* if she should have sexual relations with another at some point during the remainder of her life. Jesus simply states that by virtue of being a put away woman she *is* caused to be an adulteress. The implication of the teaching is that she becomes such regardless of what the future may hold with respect to her relationships.

Again, the operative assumption in the traditional interpretation is that adultery is strictly limited to a sexual act. It also assumes that any and all future sexual activity of one who is divorced is illicit, and thus sinful. It assumes further that no one is truly capable of controlling their sexual appetites or of remaining celibate. A lot of *assumptions* are thus required, few of which are even rational, in order to promote a theology never even suggested by the Lord.

> CASE HISTORY — *Betty, who was 75 years old, was divorced by her husband Jason, who was 81. Just a couple of years earlier they had celebrated their golden wedding anniversary. The divorce took everyone by surprise. Jason gave no other reason than he felt he would rather spend his final years alone. All efforts to bring about a reconciliation were met with stubborn resistance. Betty lived alone for the next five years at which time she met Robert, an 85 year old widower. They loved one another's company, and in time grew to love one another. Neither was interested in a sexual relationship; indeed, Robert, due to a physical condition, was incapable of one; however, they decided to marry and provide each other with warm, loving companionship during the remaining years of their lives.*

At what point did Betty become an adulteress? Was the second marriage a case of "living in adultery?" If adultery is strictly a sexual act, neither were in much danger of ever committing it. Suppose, instead of meeting and marrying Robert, Betty lived five more years after being divorced and then died without ever having had, or even having desired, a relationship with another man. Again, one inquires: at what point did she become an adulteress?! Jesus clearly teaches, or so it seems, that when Jason divorced Betty he caused her to become an adulteress. If that is true, then one must necessarily conclude that "adultery" is not limited merely to an illicit sexual act. All of this seems very confusing, but the explanation is actually very simple.

In most English language translations Jesus is purported to teach that the husband who divorces his wife causes her to "commit adultery." Grammatically, this is worded in the *active voice*, which indicates the divorced woman is the one actually committing the adultery. In the Greek text, however, this particular verb appears in the *passive voice*, which clearly signifies adultery is being committed upon or against this divorced woman. "Voice" refers to that quality of verbs which indicates the nature of the relationship of the subject to the action. The active voice indicates the subject is doing the acting; the passive voice indicates the subject is being acted upon by someone or something else.

In other words, the divorced woman in Jesus' teaching is not actually or actively engaged in doing anything; something is being done *to* her! She is here depicted by the Lord as a victim; she is being sinned against. Jesus is not declaring this woman guilty of an act of adultery; rather, He declares an act of adultery has been committed against her. This, incidentally, is exactly what is being stated in the Mark passage: "Anyone who divorces his wife and marries another woman commits adultery against her." Although some interpret this to mean the man is sinning against the second wife by having sex with her, such a view again falls victim to a host of problems evolving out of several previously examined unwarranted assumptions.

By comparing the passages in Matthew and Mark, one can quickly perceive that Jesus conveys the same truth in both: the divorced woman has had something committed *against* her, and that something is adultery! Through no stated fault of her own, this woman has been victimized. Her marriage has been terminated, and she will forever be stigmatized by this wrong that was inflicted upon her. "Moicheia" signifies the ultimate breakdown of a covenant relationship, and in this case it is a breakdown that has been forced upon another.

Her life will now be spent with a dark cloud, of her former husband's making, hanging over her head; she will live with the negative stigma of "divorced woman" attached to her. In future years she will continue to find herself in the position of having to explain her situation to those who would presume to sit in judgment upon her. A crime of far reaching proportions has been committed against her. By dissolving their covenant of marriage, the husband has committed adultery against her! The only *exception* to this, as Matthew 5:32 points out, would be if the divorced wife were the one who brought that action against herself by some infidelity against her husband and the covenant she had made with him. Again, one perceives the significance of the exception clause.

As mentioned earlier in this study, one can quickly see how vital it is that verb forms in the original text be correctly identified and translated. By rendering this verb as though it appeared in the *active* voice, interpreters of this mistranslation have been led to ascribe some of the most appalling teachings to the lips of the Lord. Armed with this false doctrine, men have labeled, libeled, castigated, and inflicted even further pain upon those already agonizing from the afflictions of a faithless spouse. The verb is not active; it is *passive*! The divorced woman is guilty of nothing! She is a victim! To victimize her further, in the name of "sound doctrine," is unconscionable!

The fact that this verb appears in the passive voice rather than the active has long been recognized, and many distinguished scholars have bemoaned the failure of translators and interpreters to correctly render it. Writing almost 300 years ago, the noted commentator Matthew Henry stated, "It is adultery *against* the wife he puts away, it is a wrong *to* her, and a breach of his contract with her." R.C.H. Lenski observes that what the "passive voice states is that this woman has been forced into a position that appears to men as though she, too, had violated the commandment not to commit adultery. She is an unfortunate woman whose marriage has been disrupted without guilt on her part" [*An Interpretation of St. Matthew's Gospel*, p. 234].

Thus, Jesus has not condemned this put away spouse of anything. No guilt has been ascribed to her; indeed, she has been sinned *against*. The responsibility for the breakdown of the covenant relationship rests solely upon the one initiating the divorce, although the stigma of that action will forever be attached to the one put away. It is this adulterous action against the victimized woman that Jesus comments upon in these two passages.

#3 — THOSE WHO MARRY A DIVORCED PERSON. "Anyone who marries the divorced woman commits adultery" [Matthew 5:32]. Although the latter part of this phrase is translated as though it was originally penned in the active voice, it should be noted the *passive* voice is used in the original text. Thus, as was true of the put away woman previously discussed, this man was not actively committing anything; something was being committed against him. He was the recipient of the action, not the one performing it. He, as well as the put away woman he married, must suffer the stigma forced upon them by the action of the first husband.

It is unfortunate, and also unfair, that those who marry one who is divorced are sometimes viewed with suspicion. Far too many begin to speculate as to the possible role that individual may have played in the breakup of the previous marriage. Although such behavior does indeed occur all too frequently, it is nevertheless not true in every case. But, such is the nature of the stigma placed upon this couple. The passive voice indicates the put away wife, and any man she may marry in the future, are both affected by the wrongful actions of the first husband. They are victims, not victimizers. Jesus neither indicts nor condemns either of them. Neither was in any way responsible for the dissolution of the first covenant of marriage. They were not in the wrong; rather, it was they who had been wronged.

At this juncture a word must be said about the statement of Jesus in Luke 16:18. "The man who marries a divorced woman commits adultery." Unlike the Matthew 5:32 passage, in which the passive voice is used, the Lord's declaration here utilizes the *active* voice. Therefore, Jesus is clearly stating that this particular man is not being victimized by the actions of the first husband, but rather he himself is guilty of committing adultery.

As one might expect, this has led to a tremendous amount of confusion and debate among biblical scholars. Why did Jesus, in this singular instance, choose to switch from the use of the passive voice to the active? A few regard this as nothing less than a glaring contradiction in the Lord's teaching with regard to one who marries a divorced person. In Matthew He declares the man innocent; in Luke He declares him guilty. Which is it?!

Others view this passage with a certain sense of satisfaction; regarding it as proof positive that all second marriages are adulterous; a justification of their hard-line theology. This position, however, fails to take into consideration that only the *man* is said to be guilty of adultery by marrying a divorced woman. The divorced woman who marries him is not condemned at all. According to all the tenets of the traditional view, the woman would be far more guilty in this situation than the man. Since it is claimed God recognizes no divorce, and since adultery is said to be strictly a sex act, she would be having an adulterous relationship with one other than her husband. The man, on the other hand, may never have been married before. Thus, he would only be guilty of engaging in an act of fornication (according to the traditional distinction between the two terms: fornication being illicit sexual activity by single people, adultery being illicit sexual activity by married people). Why then is he accused of adultery, and not the woman who is supposedly cheating on her husband? As can be quickly seen, the traditional position simply presents too many inconsistencies and leaves too many questions unanswered to merit any serious consideration.

Other scholars believe this to be a textual problem. Apparently, according to their scenario, some scribe who was making a copy of Luke's Gospel mistakenly gave this verb an active ending rather than the correct passive form. Thus, the original text would have been in agreement with the other teaching of Christ, as recorded in the other gospel records, and there is in reality no contradiction at all. Others argue that the active form in Luke's account is the correct one, and all the other gospel records were copied incorrectly. Thus, either way, it is all the fault of some careless scribe.

Unfortunately for this view, there is simply no textual evidence whatsoever that even remotely indicates these passages may have been copied incorrectly, either one way or the other. Regardless of the effort by some to prove the contrary, it appears the single use of the active voice in Luke's account was intentional. Jesus chose to use the active rather than the passive here for some specific purpose; thus, it behooves the reader to make an effort to determine that intention.

The solution to this apparent conflict in the Lord's teaching with regard to a man who marries a divorced woman lies in an examination of the contexts within which these seemingly contradictory statements occur. In the accounts of Matthew and Mark, Jesus was dealing specifically, and at some length, with the issue of divorce and remarriage. In Luke's account, however, one finds only a brief, passing reference to it, with no further commentary upon the statement supplied in the text. This in itself has caused a few scholars to speculate that perhaps this particular passage was inserted into the text by a much later copyist, and that the statement was never actually a part of the original text. It does indeed seem out of place, until one examines the context and perceives the message the Lord sought to convey, and to whom He sought to convey it.

In Matthew 5, in the Sermon on the Mount, Jesus spoke to His disciples about the importance of one's relationships, of which marriage was one of the more important, and of living one's life on a higher spiritual plane than that of the world, which had lost sight of God's IDEAL. In Matthew 19 and Mark 10, Jesus was being challenged by a group who sought to entrap Him through a discussion of the lawfulness of divorce and what constituted "just cause" for divorce. In Luke 16, however, the focus is entirely different. Jesus was not dealing with the issue of divorce and remarriage at all, nor was it brought up by those to whom He was speaking. It was mentioned only in passing as an illustration relevant to an entirely different message He was seeking to convey.

The Lord's audience in Luke 16 were Pharisees [vs. 14], who at this time were "sneering at Jesus" because of His teachings. Although they professed themselves to be righteous leaders of God's chosen people, they were in fact exceedingly worldly in both their attitudes and actions. Their hearts had become hardened toward God and their fellow men; their consciences were seared over. Their religion was little more than a pretense; a hollow shell; a public display of self-righteous ceremonialism. They were whitewashed tombs filled with death and decay. "On the outside you appear to people as righteous, but on the inside you are full of hypocrisy and wickedness" [Matthew 23:28]. They had progressed so far away from God that their behavior was in some cases even more deplorable than that of the pagan peoples about them. "You travel over land and sea to win a single convert, and when he becomes one, you make him twice as much a son of hell as you are" [Matthew 23:15]. To maintain the pretense of being pious religious leaders, however, they sought to justify their ungodly practices in any way they could. "You are the ones who justify yourselves in the eyes of men, but God knows your hearts. What is highly valued among men is detestable in God's sight" [Luke 16:15].

Among the many abuses of which these religious pretenders were guilty, perhaps the most despicable was their behavior toward women. "You devour widows' houses and for a show make lengthy prayers" [Matthew 23:14]. In situations similar to the one described in Micah 2:9, the Pharisees were casting women and children out of their homes and into the streets in order to acquire their possessions. They maintained a religious veneer for appearance's sake, but they were completely neglecting the weightier matters of God's Law: Justice, mercy and faithfulness [Matthew 23:23]. They were treating women as if they were little more than property to be bought and sold, or bartered away. Marriage had been cheapened and trivialized, and God's IDEAL had been all but forgotten. Relationship hopping; jumping in and out of marriages; had become the norm. A woman was used and discarded; new ones acquired and then cast aside; with the cycle repeating itself endlessly. Men would pass their jettisoned wives back and forth among themselves like some collectible commodity. "Love 'em and leave 'em" was the rule of the day.

These religious leaders should have been publicly displaying the IDEAL to the people through the example of their own marriage relationships. Instead, they were perhaps the worst offenders of all. They were not entering into their marriages with permanency uppermost in their minds; the concept of these unions being in any way a sacred covenant was distant from their thinking. "I'll get all I can out of her, and when I'm through with her or tire of her, I'll send her away for someone else to have, and I'll find another mate." Their minds were inclined toward the breakdown of a relationship before it was ever entered. In their hearts, they had already determined that a relationship would last only so long as they derived some personal pleasure from it. In short, the Pharisees had lost sight of God's will for their lives.

It was the ungodly nature of the Pharisees' overall behavior that Jesus addressed in Luke 16. The focus of the Lord was *not* divorce and remarriage, as it had been in Matthew and Mark, rather He was spotlighting the abusive and destructive nature of the Pharisees in general, of which their attitude toward women and marriage was merely one of many such negative qualities. Jesus informed these offenders, in Luke 16:18, that when they went from one woman to another, as they were doing; divorcing one and then marrying another, only to repeat the cycle later; they were "committing adultery." They were actively engaged in destroying one relationship after another, and for this wicked practice Jesus tells them it is *they*, not the women they are using and abusing by continually marrying, divorcing, and remarrying, who must bear the guilt for violated vows and broken covenants. This passage is far more a rebuke of the Pharisees, and their wicked actions and attitudes, than any attempt at the formulation of a comprehensive doctrinal position with respect to divorce and remarriage.

When one understands to whom our Lord addressed His statement in Luke 16:18, and the nature of their many abuses against others, the use of the active voice makes perfect sense. When speaking to those who had been victimized, Jesus utilized the passive voice; when speaking to those who were victimizers, He accurately used the active voice. With such a perception, it is clear that there is absolutely no contradiction in the teaching of the Lord with regard to this issue.

It should be noted that in each of the three major areas discussed by the Lord, it was the ultimate breakdown of the covenant of marriage that concerned Him, and all of His statements were designed to demonstrate who must bear the guilt and responsibility for that severed relationship. For anyone to attempt to construct a complex theology of divorce and remarriage that goes beyond this is to build upon the foundation of one's own opinions and traditions, rather than upon the simple truths conveyed by the Lord Jesus Christ.

The teaching of God's Son with regard to divorce and remarriage is really not as complicated as some have attempted to make it. There is an IDEAL to which all are called, and for which all must diligently strive. Any failure to do so, regardless of the cause, is a falling short of the mark. When a covenant of marriage is broken, someone has sinned, and someone must bear the guilt and responsibility for that disunion. Also, when covenants of marriage are violated and voided, innocent people are harmed. A message of hope must be conveyed, and efforts

135

to heal must be initiated.

In the gospel records, Jesus examines divorce and remarriage from several perspectives in order to convey where God places the guilt in these different case scenarios. His teaching is the epitome of simplicity; straightforward and uncomplicated; if we will allow it to be! It is only when men trample through the crystal clear waters of His teaching that those teachings become muddied!

MAY THE DIVORCED REMARRY?

The question invariably arises as to whether Jesus has made any definitive statement concerning the "legal right" of a divorced person, whether they be the innocent or guilty party, to remarry. Would God view such a remarriage as sinful, or would it be an acceptable union in His sight?

Although the apostle Paul gives some insight into this matter, as will be discussed in the next chapter, Jesus Himself remains silent. One should note, however, that Jesus does consistently refer to all second unions as marriage, and nothing less. They are never termed "living in sin" or "living in adultery." Such phrases are common among men, but are never uttered by the Lord, nor by any of His inspired writers.

Some theologians theorize that the innocent party may acceptably remarry, but the guilty party may not. Others adamantly declare that neither may remarry. Both state far more than Jesus! God's Son spoke of both innocent and guilty parties remarrying, and always spoke of those unions in terms which characterized them as legitimate marriages. Jesus neither condemned nor condoned those unions by any direct teaching; He merely acknowledged their reality: A first marriage had been terminated, and a second marriage had been initiated.

The prohibiting of marriage to any or all parties involved in a divorce simply cannot be justified by an appeal to the teaching of Jesus Christ. Such restrictions find their source and support only in the minds of men.

Chapter 7
The Teaching of the Apostle Paul

The New Testament canon is comprised of twenty-seven separate works, written by at least eight different men over a period spanning half a century. Thirteen of these inspired documents (fourteen, if one regards the epistle to the Hebrews as being from his pen) were produced by the apostle Paul. In light of the bulk of his contribution to the written revelation of God, it is no surprise that his teaching has had a tremendous impact upon the theology of the church. Virtually every area of faith, practice and worship bear the imprint of his insight.

Nevertheless, with respect to the subject of divorce and remarriage, Paul has relatively little to say. On only three occasions does this inspired apostle to the nations specifically share his views on this matter. The most extensive treatment is found about midway through his first epistle to the church in Corinth. A much less expansive discussion is found in the letter addressed to the saints in Rome. The only remaining passages which shed any light at all on this subject are found in the Pastoral Epistles, in the passages dealing with the qualities essential to spiritual leadership within the church.

Although it is true Paul's examination of this issue is not extensive, his insights are nevertheless vital to the people of God, and must be carefully studied in conjunction with the teaching of Jesus Christ.

THE EPISTLE TO THE CHURCH IN ROME

In the year 753 B.C. the city of Rome was founded, and by the time of the ministry of the apostle Paul it had become one of the most populated, prosperous and powerful cities in the world. Various estimates place the number of inhabitants anywhere between one and four million, many of whom were slaves. The city was a melting pot for immigrants of every nation, thus lending itself as a center for a wide variety of religious beliefs and practices. If ever there was a mission field desperately in need of the teachings of the Christian faith, it was Rome. Paul, aware of this need, had a strong desire to journey there and proclaim the gospel message and encourage the saints already in residence [Romans 1:13; 15:23].

Little is known about the origin of the Lord's church in Rome, although at the time Paul penned his epistle to them it had apparently been active for quite some time. Indeed, he commended them for their great faith, which "is being reported all over the world" [Romans 1:8]. Paul wrote to them from the city of Corinth during the latter part of his third missionary journey; probably in late February or early March of 58 A.D. This epistle has the distinction of being the most formal and theological of all Paul's inspired writings, discussing virtually every aspect of the Christian faith. The great reformer Martin Luther (1483-1546) characterized this epistle as "the chief part of the New Testament and the very purest Gospel." The noted Christian historian Philip Schaff observed, "It is the most remarkable production of the most remarkable man. It is his heart. It contains his theology, theoretical and practical, for which he lived and died."

The passage in the epistle to the Roman church relevant to the study of divorce and remarriage is Romans 7:1-6. In the previous chapter Paul discussed at length the fact that Christians have been set free. In Christ, one no longer dwells under Law, but lives in grace; no longer is one dead in his sins, but spiritually alive; no longer slaves of lawlessness, but servants of righteousness; no longer under the curse of death, but heirs of life everlasting. Paul proclaims the marvelous message of spiritual freedom and changed relationships; a message illustrated in a variety of ways, one of which touches upon the subject under consideration in this study.

In the Romans 7:1-6 passage, Paul indicates that mankind had at one time been bound to the old Law. This state of existence is likened to a woman being bound for life to her husband by virtue of her covenant of marriage with him. Before mankind could "legally" enter into a new relationship, the first union to which they were bound must be severed. Paul indicates the agent which accomplished this release from the first union was death, through which freedom was secured to effect a second relationship. Just as a woman is freed from her covenant of marriage by the death of her husband, so also is mankind freed by a death from the covenant of the old Law and made available for a new union.

"So, my brothers, you also died to the law through the body of Christ, that you might belong to another, to Him who was raised from the dead, in order that we might bear fruit to God. For when we were controlled by the sinful nature, the sinful passions aroused by the law were at work in our bodies, so that we bore fruit for death. But now, by dying to what once bound us, we have been released from the law so that we serve in the new way of the Spirit, and not in the old way of the written code" [Romans 7:4-6].

Those who in faith accept Christ, and are obediently "baptized into His death," are then raised to "live a new life," just as Jesus arose from the grave to renewed life [Romans 6:4]. It is a spiritual existence "in Christ" in which the devoted disciple is freed from his previous bondage to the Law. It is a new relationship, a new union, established upon a new covenant. One's bond with the world has been severed; a death has occurred; the obedient believer is free!

To illustrate this marvelous truth wrought by God's grace, Paul refers to a point of law with which his Roman readers would undoubtedly have been very familiar, "For I am speaking to men who know the law" [Romans 7:1]. The law was binding upon an individual only for as long as that person was alive. This fact was clearly displayed in the various Jewish laws governing marriage, in which a woman was bound to her husband for as long as he lived. The death of the husband, however, brought a release; freedom from his authority over her was secured. These various laws reflected the Creator's original intent for the marriage relationship, His IDEAL: a man and woman would unite with one another in a covenant of marriage so sacred and sublime that only death could dissolve it!

It should be observed additionally that the Jewish concept of marriage, and this was reflected in their laws, included the full authority of the husband over the wife; a control that was absolute. It hardly needs pointing out that in some cases this authority was greatly abused, with women suffering tremendous mistreatment and indignity as a result. A part of this "legal power" of a man over a woman was the prerogative of a man to initiate a divorce against his wife for virtually any cause. The woman, however, was not granted the same right by Jewish law. Although some later exercised it anyway, like Salome, it was in defiance of the accepted norm of their society.

By law, there were only two avenues of release from a covenant of marriage open to a woman: if her husband issued her a certificate of divorce or if he died. Although the latter was the IDEAL, God permitted the former due to the hardness of heart and extreme cruelty of many of His people. Aside from these two, there was no legal recourse for the woman; she was bound to her husband for life. Of course, there were other less legal options — murder, for example — but such alternatives carried severe consequences, which rendered them unthinkable to all but the most desperate or unbalanced. The simple reality of Jewish law was that if a woman, for whatever reason, desired to be released from her covenant of marriage, and her husband refused to grant such a release, she had no legal option but to remain his wife until such time as either he or she died.

Upon the death of the husband, however, the wife was at that point "released from the law of marriage" [Romans 7:2]. More literally, the original Greek text states: "…from the law of the man/husband." Again, one detects the nature of the absolute authority the man was given over the woman by Jewish law and custom. An example of this control is clearly seen in Numbers 30:8 where a husband was even entitled by law to nullify his wife's vows to God if in his judgment they were inappropriate. The Jewish "law of the man/husband" allowed this authority in all areas of the marital relationship.

Yet another indication of the nature of this "law of the man/husband," at least from the wife's perspective, is revealed in the wording of Romans 7:1. "Do you not know, brothers — for I am speaking to men who know the law — that the law has authority over a man only as long as he lives." The word translated "authority" is "kurieuo," which comes from the root word meaning "lord," and conveys the concept of someone "lording it over" someone or something else. The law "lorded it over" mankind until death set them free from that dominion. On the cross Jesus Christ would secure that freedom for all men through His death, thus allowing men to live in freedom rather than in slavery to law [Colossians 2:14].

Just as the law lorded it over the lives of men, so also did some men derive perverse pleasure in lording it over others, and in exercising authority [Matthew 20:25; Luke 22:25]. There were far too many men during the time of the apostle Paul who were "lording it over" their wives. They perceived themselves as the absolute monarch of all their domain, and, tragically, they counted their wives as being among their lowly subjects. Thus, they behaved irresponsibly in their role as leader of the household.

In Romans 7:2 Paul simply states a well-known point of law: the wife was regarded as being under the legal lordship of her husband for life; a dominion from which she was legally helpless to extricate herself. Should she determine in her heart to circumvent law by leaving her husband and joining herself to another, she would be guilty of breaking covenant with her husband. "So then, if she marries another man while her husband is still alive, she is called an adulteress. But if her husband dies, she is released from the law and is not an adulteress, even though she marries another man" [vs. 3]. By severing her relationship with her husband, either by abandoning him or divorcing him, so as to seek out a relationship with another, this woman brought down upon herself the characterization "adulteress." The guilt for the destruction of the covenant of marriage must be borne by her, since it was she who initiated the disunion. Because of her action she would be called an adulteress.

Indeed, "adulteress" would probably be one of the kinder labels affixed to this woman. Any woman who took it upon herself to violate societal and cultural norms was a marked woman. She would be viewed with horror, and strictly avoided, by all "decent" citizens. How one was *perceived* by society could greatly affect how one was *received* by society.

It was partly with such concerns in mind that Paul gave the instructions he did with regard to women in Corinth wearing a veil [1 Corinthians 11:2-16]. It was "a sign of authority on her head" [vs. 10], a visible demonstration of her willingness to accept her role and place in God's order, and her willingness to live according to the norms of the current customs of the society within which she resided.

Please don't misunderstand Paul here! He is *not* voicing his agreement with the prevalent Jewish concept of a husband having the legal right to lord it over his wife, nor is he condoning the many abuses which took place under this "law of the man/husband." Paul is most definitely *not* implying that women are in some way inferior to men; a lesser part of God's creation. If anyone could ever be applauded for his advocacy of the inherent rights of women, it was the apostle Paul.

Paul was neither condemning nor condoning anything. He merely sought to use a well-known law, the particulars of which were common knowledge and widely accepted in society, to illustrate a particular spiritual truth he hoped to impress upon their minds. In a similar vein, Paul spoke of the practice of baptism for the dead [1 Corinthians 15:29], neither condemning nor condoning it, but merely using it as an illustration to impress upon the minds of his readers a greater spiritual truth. Thus, from his lack of discussion one certainly does not infer his approval of such a doctrine; he merely utilized a practice not unfamiliar to his readers to illustrate a much deeper reality.

Isn't it rather strange, he asks the Corinthian brethren, for someone to practice baptism for the dead if they do not even believe in the resurrection? If the latter is false doctrine, as some claimed, then the former was a futile practice. In the Romans 7 passage, Paul used the "law of the man/husband" to illustrate a situation in life wherein one party is bound to another with absolutely no hope of legal extrication short of a death. By drawing upon their knowledge of this law, his readers might better understand the truth that they were incapable of extricating themselves from the abusive lordship of law and sin over their lives. Until a death occurred, they would never be free to be joined to another.

The point Paul ultimately seems to be making in this passage is that there are some things in life to which all are at some point bound, and from which one is incapable of effecting one's own release. For a woman, at that particular time and place in history, this truth was largely reflected in the restrictive parameters of "the law of the man/husband." Like the woman with no legal recourse, all men were bound in a relationship with sin; in bondage to law; with no way to secure their own release. However, through death (Christ's death on the cross, and their own sharing in that death through a visible demonstration of their faith [baptism] — Romans 6:3f) they were set free from bondage. Given a new lease on life, by virtue of their death to the first relationship, they could now join themselves to another in a spiritually satisfying union.

As one examines the teaching of the Romans 7 passage, it becomes increasingly evident that Paul is not actually discussing the issue of divorce and remarriage at all. Thus, to view this text as a doctrinal decree binding upon the people of the new dispensation is to utterly fail to perceive the intent of his teaching here. Those who insist Paul's statement should be regarded as church doctrine face a host of difficult problems. The decree is rather one-sided, first of all, since restrictions are placed only upon the women and not upon the men. Further, does one really want to begin governing the practices of the church based upon the authority of Jewish laws, customs and traditions? For anyone to utilize an illustration taken from such sources to formulate a doctrine binding upon those who are free in Christ is unsound, and it paves the way for further such unwarranted outside intrusions and legalistic impositions. By focusing entirely upon Paul's illustration from law, rather than upon the marvelous message of grace which he sought to convey more clearly by use of this example, men have drawn some highly erroneous conclusions.

Some, for example, have cited this passage as proof positive that once a covenant of marriage has been established it is absolutely impossible for that covenant ever to be dissolved except by the death of one of the covenantal parties. Thus, they reason, all marriages are for life, and no divorce will ever truly be sanctioned or recognized by God. If the first husband is still alive, and the woman leaves him and marries another man, then she is committing adultery.

Such a position fails to consider several significant points in this passage, however. Although some translations do indeed speak of the woman "marrying" another man, it should be pointed out that in the original text Paul does not use the Greek word for marriage. When a writer sought to convey the concept "to marry," the usual Greek word employed was "gameo." In all of the passages from the Gospel records in which Jesus spoke of people divorcing and "marrying," it was this word that He used. However, the word employed by Paul in Romans 7:3 is "ginomai," which means "to become." It seems to convey, when used in connection with relationships, the idea of becoming attached to or being with someone in a close personal association. For a married woman to associate that closely, perhaps even intimately, with another man was considered extremely inappropriate behavior. This may seem somewhat old-fashioned in light of the proliferation of very close personal, professional and social associations between married members of the opposite sex in today's world, but it was a significant breach of the social norm of the ancient world. To transgress that norm could quickly cause a woman to be "called an adulteress," even though no sexual misbehavior may have taken place.

The point Paul makes in this illustration is that the woman was party to a binding covenant, and thus must behave accordingly. The formation of any kind of close association with another man, even though no sexual intimacies transpired between them, was viewed at that time as overstepping the parameters of one's covenant of marriage. Following the death of her husband, however, the woman was then free to associate with whomever she desired, without incurring any subsequent stigmas or labels.

Thus, it is an extremely large assumption for one to dogmatically declare Paul is here speaking of a woman *marrying* another man. The word for marriage is not even used. Far more likely is that Paul is depicting a *close association* between a married woman and another man; one that would be regarded as far too bold a relationship for a married woman in that day and age. In a similar vein, one cannot truly associate with the Lord in a close relationship, much less enjoy betrothal with

Him, while still married to the world. A complete severing of the first relationship must occur before one is free to enjoy a second union. Assuming this woman in Romans 7 did indeed leave her husband and associate herself with another man, perhaps even sexually, it would not legally be regarded as a marriage because the first covenant had not been officially terminated. Thus, Paul's use of the term "being with" someone, rather than "to marry," still applies.

One also assumes far more than Scripture specifically declares when they state *death* is the *only* means whereby a covenant of marriage may be recognized by both God and man as being terminated. The Bible clearly teaches God permitted, though reluctantly, and recognized the dissolution of a marriage by means of divorce. There is no question but what it fell far short of the IDEAL, and God was far from pleased with the breakdown of the covenant, and those who were guilty of destroying the relationship would be held responsible. However, the reality of such tragedies was acknowledged, and when subsequent relationships were entered into they were deemed marriages, both in the eyes of man and God. Paul even declares to the saints in Corinth that when the divorced remarry they are *not* guilty of sin [1 Corinthians 7:27-28]. All of this would be completely inconsistent with and contradictory to Romans 7 if indeed Paul was declaring death to be the *only* permitted cause for the ending of a covenant of marriage, and the *only* method whereby one was truly free to enter into a second marital union.

As previously mentioned, the common Greek word for "marriage" is "*gameo*." In Romans 7:2, however, one discovers Paul uses yet another term in the phrase "by law a *married* woman is bound to her husband... ." The word employed by Paul in this text for "married" is "*hupandros*," which means "under a man." This was legal terminology signifying one was under the authority and power of another. This further emphasizes the fact that Paul was not so much seeking to depict a normal, IDEAL marital relationship, as he was stressing the concept of the "law of the man/husband," which was viewed as a legal dominion of the man over the woman. It was this idea of lordship over and domination of another, and the complete lack of power of the party in subjection to extricate themselves from that authoritative control, that Paul spoke of in Romans 7; *not* as condoning it, but rather utilizing it to illustrate a vital spiritual truth.

Paul, in this message to the saints in the city of Rome, was not seeking to convey some aspect of the IDEAL with regard to the covenant of marriage. Instead, he proclaimed one of the many harsh realities of Jewish law and custom which served to control one segment of the populace; in this case: wives. This dominion was at times oppressive and cruel, if her husband was not a godly man, and, from a legal perspective, the wife was powerless to effect her release. The development of a detailed theology of divorce and remarriage binding upon every member of the present dispensation of grace was not even remotely the intent of the apostle Paul in this passage. Neither should it be ours.

THE FIRST EPISTLE TO THE CHURCH IN CORINTH

The site upon which the city of Corinth would later be built was one of the very first regions in Greece to become inhabited. It was a natural crossroads for both commerce and travel from all parts of the known world. This ancient city also had the distinction of being situated near two separate seaports by which it was serviced: Cenchrea to the east on the Aegean Sea, and Lechaeum to the north on the Gulf of Corinth. In 146 B.C. the city was completely destroyed by the Roman General Lucius Mummius, but because of its strategic location it was rebuilt in 46 B.C. by Julius Caesar. Following its reconstruction it was given the name Corinth. By the time Paul wrote his epistle to the church there, the city had grown to a population of over 600,000 individuals, about two-thirds of whom were slaves.

During the first century A.D., Corinth had come to be regarded as the place to go if one desired to "have a good time." Some scholars have characterized it as one of the most wicked cities in the realm. It even became a common term of derision to refer to someone as a "Corinthian," indicating that they had given themselves over to the many lusts and vices of the flesh. To accuse another of "Corinthianizing," was to accuse them of prostitution. This reputation of unrestrained sensuality was even incorporated into the religions of the area. The famed Temple of Aphrodite was located here, which boasted of hundreds of cult prostitutes with whom the religious could engage in various acts of "worship." It would be quite an understatement to say Corinth was a city that did *not* enjoy a favorable reputation.

With regard to the establishment of the church in Corinth, it had its beginnings through the work of Paul near the end of his second missionary journey. This would place the birth of the body of believers in that location about the year 53 A.D. The biblical account of its origin can be read in Acts 18:1-18. After Paul's departure from Corinth, an eloquent man named Apollos labored to nourish and develop this young congregation [Acts 18:27 - 19:1].

Paul penned this first of two preserved epistles to his children in the faith in Corinth from the city of Ephesus sometime during the winter of 56-57 A.D. Therefore, this work was written and sent out a little over a year *prior* to the composition of the epistle to the church in Rome. As one can easily see, less than four years had elapsed between the establishment of the church in Corinth and the writing of this rather lengthy letter to them. Thus, spiritually speaking, they could certainly not be characterized as a mature body of believers; there was simply insufficient time for such growth to have occurred — a fact evident in both the tone and content of the epistle. These recent converts to Christ Jesus were beset with numerous questions about their new-found faith, and how to apply Christian principles to the challenges of daily life in an immoral environment. Paul sought to address these various areas of personal struggle in a very practical manner in this epistle; indeed, some have called it the most practical of all his writings.

Many of the questions and concerns of the Corinthians involved their interpersonal relationships. Perhaps the most delicate and sensitive of these were tackled head-on by Paul in chapter seven: religiously mixed marriages, advice to virgins and widows, and the issue of marriage, divorce and remarriage. Paul, very methodically and logically, addressed each of these areas at great length, resulting in the most intensive and extensive treatment of these matters found anywhere in the New Covenant writings. Thus, it behooves one to carefully examine each of the groups to whom Paul addressed himself in this chapter, and to note the inspired advice he gives to each.

#1 — TROUBLE AMONG MARRIED BELIEVERS.

"To the married I give this command (not I, but the Lord): A wife must not separate from her husband. But if she does, she must remain unmarried or else be reconciled to her husband. And a husband must not divorce his wife" [1 Corinthians 7:10-11]. One should not overlook the fact that the apostle Paul is speaking to a specific group of individuals in this text: married believers. In the five verses which immediately follow, he addresses his thoughts to "the rest" — believers who find themselves married to unbelievers (religiously mixed marriages). Understanding to whom these various statements are being made will help one to more fully appreciate, and more correctly interpret, the teaching of Paul.

Although Paul on occasion, during the course of his instruction to the church in Corinth, indicates that his advice falls under the heading of personal preference (opinion), it is important to note that in this first statement dealing with troubled marriages he clearly declares the source of the teaching to be from the Lord.

It is the will of the Lord God, Paul informs these married believers, that "a wife must not separate from her husband" [vs. 10]. The word translated "separate" is the Greek verb "*chorizo*," which means "to sever, disunite, put asunder, divide, separate." Some have suggested an actual divorce is not in view here, merely a temporary separation. This seems unlikely in light of Paul's statement in the next verse: "But if she does (become separated from him), let her remain unmarried." Paul obviously regarded them as being "unmarried" following the "putting asunder, severing, disunion" of their marital relationship.

Further validation of the position that this is indeed a termination of the covenant of marriage, and not merely a temporary separation while the marriage remains in force, is seen in Paul's choice of words. He begins the statement by saying, "To the married…" [vs. 10]. This is the

Greek word "gameo," the common word depicting the state of marriage. Then, following the act signified by "chorizo," he said, "But if she does, she must remain unmarried..." [vs. 11], which utilizes the Greek word "agamos." In the Greek language one negates a word by prefixing the letter alpha ("a") to it. Thus, the word "agamos" signifies the *negation* of the state of marriage; it has become a state of *non-marriage*. The couple has severed their marriage; their union has been dissolved; a division has occurred; a state of marriage no longer exists between this former husband and wife.

Another fact which is vital to note is that "*chorizo*" appears in the *passive* voice, rather than the active, in both of its occurrences within this passage. Look at the text again: "To the married I give this command (not I, but the Lord): A wife must not separate from her husband. But if she does {literally, the Greek reads: "But if indeed she should be separated"}, she must remain unmarried or else be reconciled to her husband. And a husband must not divorce his wife" [vs. 10-11]. This passage is often translated as if Paul used the *active* voice with this verb. However, he does not! The text is more correctly translated: "A wife must not *be separated* from her husband. But if she should *be separated...*." This phrases the statement in the *passive* voice, in which it was originally written, rather than the active. This has the effect of making this statement far less specific with regard to the responsibility and culpability for the breakdown of the covenant of marriage. By using the active voice the implication is that the woman herself is guilty of severing the relationship with her husband. However, by correctly translating the passage in the passive voice, Paul conveys the fact that it is more the *state of separation itself* that is being condemned.

God's original design was that the two become one flesh. A wife should not be separated from her husband. A husband should not be separated from his wife. "'I hate divorce,' says the Lord God of Israel" [Malachi 2:16]; it falls short of His IDEAL. The man and his wife were designed to remain united. To be separated, or disunited, is deplored by both God and Paul.

In the ancient world only the husband had the legal right to seek out a divorce; Paul says he must *not* exercise it [vs. 11]. The woman was more passive in such situations, often having a divorce imposed upon her by a cruel mate. Separation, whether actively sought out by the man, or passively experienced by the woman, was a devastating detour from God's original plan for marriage. Paul tells these believing couples that they need to keep His IDEAL uppermost in their minds.

The implication of the passage, however, is that in spite of the goal of believers to live in harmony with the will of God for their lives, trouble has somehow arisen in the marriage of two believers. Although Paul does not specifically assign responsibility for the divorce, it seems rather clear from the use of the passives with reference to the woman, and the command against husbands putting away their wives, that the woman in this illustration has probably been victimized. For whatever cause, she now finds herself in an unmarried state; she has *become* (passive voice) separated. As a Christian, what should her response be in this situation? This is really the issue Paul is addressing in this first section. Paul advises her to "remain unmarried or else be reconciled to her husband."

God's advice to this put away woman through His inspired apostle is that she focus on the goal of a reconciliation. Although she is no longer united to her husband, rather than immediately seeking out another relationship, she should first make every effort to confront the problems in her present situation and actively work for a solution. The purpose of not seeking another relationship at this time is because it would remove all hope of a possible reconciliation. Give it some time, Paul advises; who knows but what the rift in this relationship may come to be repaired.

One cannot help but think of the efforts of God Himself as He repeatedly sought to restore His relationship with His unfaithful spouse Israel. God held on to hope for a reconciliation when most would have given up in frustration. Unfortunately, as was the case with God and Israel, reconciliation isn't always realized, regardless of the time invested or the energy expended. God finally had to acknowledge the fact that His faithless spouse simply was *not* coming back to Him. At that point He turned from His efforts at reconciliation and entered into a union with her sister Judah.

Neither God nor Paul are suggesting that a put away woman must spend the rest of her life single and celibate in the hope that her husband may one day come back to her. Don't forget: God Himself did not wait forever! What is being commanded, however, is that when married believers find themselves, for whatever reason, in a state of disunion, their *first* order of business, as children of God, is to do all in their power to effect a reconciliation. The covenant of marriage is too sacred and precious to be given up on so quickly. The idea of remarriage should not even enter their minds as long as there is even a glimmer of hope that the relationship may at some point be re-established. The believer is to pursue every possible avenue, no matter how small, before finally conceding to the irreversible demise of the relationship.

To suggest, as have some, that a woman who has been divorced by her husband must remain unmarried and celibate for the rest of her life is to suggest that God in effect has delivered to this victim the knockout punch, after her husband had first dealt her the knockdown blow. Not only is such out of character with God and His written revelation, it is also inconsistent with the teaching of Paul in 1 Corinthians 7. "Now to the unmarried and the widows I say: It is good for them to stay unmarried, as I am. But if they cannot control themselves, they should marry, for it is better to marry than to burn with passion" [vs. 8-9]. Why would this passage not apply to the unmarried woman in verse 11 as well?! Some suggest that in verse 8, when using the word "unmarried" ("agamos"), Paul refers exclusively to those who have never been married. That's a rather large assumption in light of the fact that just three verses later [vs. 11] "agamos" is used to describe the state of being "unmarried" by virtue of divorce! Paul obviously did not restrict the meaning of this term to "single by virtue of never having been married" — neither should those who seek to interpret his writings.

It is true that Paul encourages the unmarried and widows to remain in that state if they are capable of doing so; especially would this be true of those "unmarried" because of divorce, so that time may be allowed for a possible reconciliation. However, if the unmarried are unable to control their sexual passions, it is far better for them to marry than to fulfill their desires in an illicit manner.

"Now for the matters you wrote about: It is good for a man not to marry. But since there is so much immorality, each man should have his own wife, and each woman her own husband" [1 Corinthians 7:1-2]. *Each* man and *each* woman! Which aspect of this passage suggests the woman in verse 11 is excluded from the principle given here? Does Paul state, "Each woman, *except* those who are divorced"? Does he write, "If they cannot control themselves, they should marry; everyone, that is, *except* the woman I'm about to discuss — let *her* burn"?

Through careful examination of the text and context, and by restraining oneself from imposing his religious biases upon the passage, one can quickly perceive the simple message conveyed by the apostle Paul. When relationships end, tremendous effort must be made to restore them; an effort that cannot and will not be made if the separated believers are eagerly seeking out new relationships. Believing spouses should not terminate their relationships. Not only are they in a covenant with one another, but as believers they are also in a covenant with God. Thus, the IDEAL should be a goal which they work together to achieve. When serious problems do arise, severe enough even to bring about a severing of the relationship, every effort must be made to solve those problems and restore the marriage. Don't even consider another relationship; focus entirely upon the one you were in. Only when all traces of hope are gone, and every potential avenue leading to reconciliation has been pursued, does the believer, like God with Israel, acknowledge the reality of their irreparable loss and move on.

#2 — TROUBLE WITHIN RELIGIOUSLY MIXED MARRIAGES.

Paul has just finished speaking to married believers who are experiencing the tragedy of a relationship gone bad. Now, in verses 12-16, he turns his attention "to the rest" — marital relationships in which only one spouse is a believer. In this case, Paul states his advice to them comes from his own wisdom; these are *his* insights and judgments. There was no direct revelation from God, nor any specific command in the Scriptures, to which he could appeal with regard to the situation he was about to address. Although Paul clearly declares these forthcoming views to be solely his own opinion, yet "I give an opinion as one who by the mercy of the Lord is trustworthy" [vs. 25], "and I think that I too have the Spirit of God" [vs. 40]. If indeed one regards Paul as trustworthy and in possession of the Holy Spirit, one should have no difficulty confidently embracing these opinions as reflections of the mind of God. Approximately eight years after Paul wrote this epistle to the church in Corinth, the apostle Peter characterized his writings as a part of "the Scriptures," stating Paul wrote according to "the wisdom that God gave him" [2 Peter 3:15-16]. Thus, one should not be too quick to discount these statements simply because Paul declares them to be his "opinions."

"To the rest I say this (I, not the Lord): If any brother has a wife who is not a believer and she is willing to live with him, he must not divorce her. And if a woman has a husband who is not a believer and he is willing to live with her, she must not divorce him" [vs. 12-13]. It should be noted that Paul, like Jesus, was aware of the fact that women were beginning to assert themselves by initiating divorces against their husbands. Such behavior certainly did not meet with the overwhelming approval of society at that time, especially among the conservative Jewish element, but the fact of its occurrence, and its frequency, was undeniable. Thus, both Jesus and Paul acknowledged their awareness of this movement within society and modified their remarks accordingly so as to make them relevant to this reality.

It should be noted at this juncture that religiously mixed marriages, although recognized by God as legitimate covenants of marriage, nevertheless fall short of the IDEAL. Ideally, the covenant people of God would form covenant relationships with one another, not with those outside of God's covenant. "Do not be yoked together with unbelievers ... What does a believer have in common with an unbeliever?" [2 Corinthians 6:14-15]. Although this command is certainly open to numerous applications, many feel it is especially pertinent to marriage, which has the distinction of being the most intimate of all our interpersonal relationships. Paul further emphasizes this principle when he instructs widows they are indeed free to remarry, "but he must belong to the Lord" [1 Corinthians 7:39]. A vital element of God's IDEAL for marriage is that husbands and wives are to be "heirs together of the grace of life" [1 Peter 3:7, *King James Version*].

In spite of God's IDEAL being repeatedly held up for display among His people, not all choose to embrace it. It is simply a fact of life that a great many believers enter into covenants of marriage with unbelievers. Such seems to have been the case with the parents of Timothy, whose mother was a Jewish believer, but whose father apparently was neither [Acts 16:1; 2 Timothy 1:5]. There are also numerous occasions where two unbelievers marry and later one of them becomes a believer. This also results in a religiously mixed marriage. It is to believers who find themselves in just such a marriage that Paul addresses himself in this particular passage.

His advice to them is: do not terminate your covenant of marriage simply because your spouse is not a believer. Such a situation does not constitute a "just cause." If an unbeliever is willing to live with a believer, and to abide by the conditions of their covenant of marriage, then a divorce must not be sought. The goal of the believing spouse, in such situations, should be to win over their unbelieving spouse, and to raise their children in an atmosphere of love and reverence for the Lord. Most interpreters feel this to be the major significance of Paul's statement in verse 14: "For the unbelieving husband has been sanctified through his wife, and the unbelieving wife has been sanctified through her believing husband. Otherwise your children would be unclean, but as it is, they are holy." Although a few have interpreted this to mean the faith of the believer will be conferred upon his/her unbelieving family at the judgment, and that they will thus be eternally saved along with the believer (since God doesn't want to break up families in heaven any more than He does on earth), this seems to be far more wishful thinking than sound exegesis.

In a sense, Paul was encouraging these believing spouses to view their families as a mission field. Rather than berating them for their religiously mixed marriages, even though they fell short of the IDEAL, he challenged them to seize this opportunity to bring their loved ones into a saving relationship with the Lord, and thus achieve the IDEAL. "How do you know, wife, whether you will save your husband? Or, how do you know, husband, whether you will save your wife?" [vs. 16].

Such should be the goal for which the believer tirelessly labors. At times the goal is realized, at times it is not, but the striving for it should never be abandoned. Eunice was successful in imparting her faith to her son Timothy, but there is no indication that she enjoyed that same success with her Greek husband. There are no guarantees of ultimate success, but without the effort there is a guarantee of failure. The apostle Peter agrees with Paul's advice to these believing spouses: "Wives, in the same way be submissive to your husbands so that, if any of them do not believe the word, they may be won over without words by the behavior of their wives, when they see the purity and reverence of your lives" [1 Peter 3:1-2].

It was partly for this reason that Paul stressed these believing spouses must not seek to terminate their marriages; they were opportunities to bring unbelieving spouses to a saving knowledge of the Lord. Some in Corinth, perhaps reflecting upon the situation among the post-captivity Jews in which they were commanded to put away their pagan wives, might have been considering the same action against their unbelieving mates. Paul instructs them that in their case this would not be a viable option; the situations were dissimilar, and therefore the solution to the former was not applicable to the latter.

Thus, the believer must not initiate a divorce simply because their mate is an unbeliever. The goal of the believer, in keeping with God's IDEAL, is to preserve the marriage. But, what if the unbelieving spouse decides to end the relationship? How is the believer to respond in such a situation? "But if the unbeliever leaves, let him do so. A believing man or woman is not bound in such circumstances; God has called us to live in peace" [vs. 15]. It is not uncommon for religiously mixed marriages to fail. The unbelieving spouse may eventually become extremely uncomfortable with the lifestyle of the believer. Their attitudes, actions and aspirations may be so completely incompatible — one being devoted to the world, the other being devoted to the Lord — that a release from the marriage is sought. If the unbeliever, for whatever reason, chooses to leave, thus ending the relationship, Paul urges the believer to allow them to do so.

A couple of things should be noticed here. First, it is the *unbeliever* who is said to initiate the severing of the union. Paul depicts the believer, who would be aware of God's IDEAL, as being unwilling to take such action. Also, it should be observed that Paul urges the believer to *allow* the disunion even though no mention is made of the unbeliever having committed an act of sexual infidelity. This would appear to be a serious contradiction of Jesus' so-called "exception clause," which some staunchly maintain allows divorce *only* if an act of sexual infidelity has occurred. Is Paul here contradicting Jesus? Is he making an exception to the exception clause?! With a proper understanding of the Lord's intent in the so-called "exception clause," however, and in light of the true meaning of "adultery," the matter is quickly resolved and one perceives there is no contradiction of teaching here whatsoever.

Nevertheless, such advice has troubled a great many people. Paul is essentially saying, "If your spouse is determined to leave, don't fight it; let them leave! Even if they have not committed sexual infidelity with another, but simply don't want to be in a relationship with a devoted disciple of the Lord — let them leave! God has called us to peaceful relationships, not to warring and fighting to preserve a relationship with someone who obviously does not desire it." Yes, efforts should be made to reconcile, pursue every option, but if the situation is beyond hope, and if reconciliation is unattainable, then let it go! For a believing mate to agonize through months of tumultuous legal wrangling to preserve what their unbelieving mate has chosen to terminate, and what was frankly less than God's IDEAL to begin with, would be foolish and futile. The advice of Paul is succinctly stated: *let them go.*

This raises some questions with regard to the status of the believer following the departure of their mate. Is the believer still considered legally married? If not, is the believer free to remarry? The answer to both these questions seems to be found in Paul's statement: "A believing man or woman *is not bound* in such circumstances" [vs. 15]. If one is no longer bound to a spouse, then a setting free has occurred. That which bound them together as one has been dissolved, and they are two once more. Clearly a severing of the covenant of marriage has occurred, at which point there is no law, from either God or man, which forbids them from seeking out a new marital relationship.

When an unbelieving spouse leaves the believer, "from that day onward the fetters of the marriage tie have been broken and remain so, now and indefinitely. The deserting spouse broke them. No law binds the believing spouse. Let us add that no odium on the part of Christians has a right to bind such a believing, deserted spouse. It goes without saying that a believing spouse will by Christian kindness and persuasion do all that can be done to prevent a rupture. But when these fail, Paul's verdict is: 'Thou art free!'" [R.C.H. Lenski, *An Interpretation of I & II Corinthians*, p. 295].

#3 — SOUND ADVICE FOR DIFFICULT TIMES. "Are you bound to a wife? Do not seek to be released. Are you released from a wife? Do not seek a wife" [1 Corinthians 7:27, *New American Standard Bible*]. With this statement Paul provides additional commentary with regard to his remark in verse 20: "Let each man remain in that condition in which he was called." The context within which these statements occur must not be overlooked; to do so is to risk reaching some rather erroneous conclusions. Paul foretells of a time of great persecution for the people of God; a difficult season fast approaching, and in some locations already present. It would be a time of tremendous affliction in which personal relationships would be severely challenged. In view of these impending circumstances Paul writes, "I think that it is good for you to remain as you are" [vs. 26]. If one happened to be a virgin, then remain in that state; if married, maintain that covenant; if divorced or widowed, don't seek out another relationship. The days ahead were going to be difficult, Paul explained, therefore don't further complicate your life. Focus on maintaining your current position in life, and your present relationships, and pray for the strength to endure the trials that lie ahead.

In verses 28-35 he further elaborates on these coming years of stressful crisis, saying in part, "I am only trying to spare you" [vs. 28], and "I want you to be free from concern" [vs. 32]. Involvement in a marital relationship would add to one's cares and concerns, and would distract one's focus and divide one's interests. In light of the difficulties soon to be unleashed upon them; years of trauma that would cause many to lose sight of their heavenly goal and forfeit their faith; Paul sought to encourage Christians to order their lives in such a way that they might remain focused completely "upon the Lord without distraction" [vs. 35].

In no way was Paul condemning the state of marriage, nor was he suggesting that those who entered in to it were engaging in sinful behavior. Paul merely expressed an opinion. It was his feeling that during times of extreme persecution and affliction, those who were married would experience greater anxieties than those who were single. His desire was simply to spare them this additional stress. In a similar vein, Jesus said, "How dreadful it will be in those days for pregnant women and nursing mothers!" [Matthew 24:19]. Jesus certainly did not oppose parenthood, or have something against children. He was simply aware of the stresses and anxieties which would have to be endured by these mothers during the time of the impending persecution.

Neither was Paul in any way encouraging those who were married to terminate their relationships, which some believe Paul taught in the latter part of verse 29: "From now on those who have wives should live as if they had none." What Paul was stressing was that those who were married should not let the many domestic obligations and concerns of their daily lives distract them from a devotion to the Lord that would carry them through the coming persecution. If they hoped to endure, their relationship with God must come first. Yes, work diligently to maintain your marriage, but don't lose sight of the Lord. A successful marriage would mean little if it came at the expense of one's relationship with God or the surrendering of one's faith. Those who are married must strive all the more, far more than one who is single, to keep the many responsibilities of life in perspective and in their proper priority; all of which becomes even more difficult during times of crisis. Thus, in the sense of one's singleness of devotion to God, be as though you had no other relationships or responsibilities. This is the message Paul sought to convey to the brethren in Corinth.

With this understanding of the context in mind, Paul's advice in verse 27 becomes much more understandable: "Are you bound to a wife? Do not seek to be released. Are you released from a wife? Do not seek a wife." Although some translations have rendered the third phrase in this verse, "Are you *unmarried?*," it is not only textually incorrect to do so, but very misleading as well. The Greek word for "unmarried," as mentioned earlier, is "agamos." That is *not* the word being used here, however. Paul uses "lusis," which means "an unbinding, a loosing, a release, to set free, to break or untie." Further, Paul adds: "From a wife." Thus, the phrase in the original text reads, "Are you unbound from a wife?" Although this certainly would result in an "unmarried" state, it was a result reached via divorce, not by virtue of the fact that one had never been married. In some translations the latter is implied by means of using the word "unmarried," and by *deleting* the phrase "from a wife." This has led some to declare divorce is *not* being discussed in this passage; a false conclusion derived from a faulty translation of the original text.

Other interpreters of this passage have suggested that the "release" being discussed by Paul is a release resulting from the death of the wife. Although this would definitely bring about the husband's "release" from his wife, there is simply nothing in the text itself to suggest such an assumption to be valid; indeed, there is much to suggest it is not. The word "lusis" appears twice in this verse, and should be translated consistently in both locations, unless there is some compelling textual or contextual justification for doing otherwise. If it is to be interpreted as meaning "a release from one's wife by means of her death" in the second occurrence, as some maintain, the laws of sound biblical interpretation require it to be so understood in the first occurrence as well, unless there is some specific, demonstrable cause to the contrary. If "lusis" is thus consistently translated in both locations according to the above interpretation, it would read, "Are you bound to a wife? Do not seek to be released by her death. Are you released from a wife by her death? Do not seek a wife." The unmistakable implication of Paul, if the above interpretation is allowed, is that he was seeking to discourage husbands from *murdering* their wives as an alternative to divorce! Although such would certainly be wrong, there is simply no evidence within the context that would justify interpreting "lusis" as signifying "release by death," nor is there anything inherent within the meaning of the word itself which would validate such a position. At best, such a stance is merely an unwarranted assumption hastily proffered; at worst, it is an intentional effort to manipulate the text so as to bolster one's personal views.

Paul neither condemns nor condones divorce in this passage, he merely acknowledges the sad reality of it. One should also not assume Paul forbids the right of remarriage to those who have been divorced. He would prefer they remain single, as he himself was, especially in light of the difficult times ahead, "But, if you do marry, you have not sinned ... But those who marry will face many troubles in this life, and I want to spare you this" [vs. 28].

This is perhaps one of the most significant passages in the New Testament writings on the subject of remarriage, and, sadly, one of the most overlooked. Is it a sin for one who is divorced to remarry? Paul unequivocally declares: *it is not.* This view is consistent, by-the-way, with the teaching of Jesus, who also did not forbid it, it is consistent with the Law of Moses, and it is consistent with the Lawgiver Himself, who not only did not forbid remarriage to His people, but practiced it Himself after divorcing faithless Israel. For one to forbid the divorced to remarry, or to declare it to be sinful, or that remarriage constitutes a state of "living in sin/adultery," is inconsistent with the teaching and practice of Paul, Jesus, the Law, the Prophets, and God. There is simply no biblical basis for such a denial of marriage to the divorced.

#4 — ADVICE TO WIDOWS. The final passage in Paul's epistle to the church in Corinth in which one finds material relevant to the focus of this study is a statement concerning widows: "A woman is bound to her husband as long as he lives. But if her husband dies, she is free to marry anyone she wishes, but he must belong to the Lord. In my judgment, she is happier if she stays as she is — and I think that I too have the Spirit of God" [1 Corinthians 7:39-40].

Paul re-emphasizes two great realities in this passage, one divine and one earthly: (1) God's IDEAL that men and women become partners for life within a covenant of marriage, and (2) the less godly concept conveyed by "the law of the man/husband," in which a woman was not just married to, but *bound* to, her husband for life, and was under his dominion and lordship, without any legal recourse for release, until the time of his death. Both of these concepts, previously discussed in some depth, can be detected in this passage.

In the present case, Paul presents a woman who lived in violation of neither. She honored her covenant of marriage until the death of her spouse; maintaining her "good standing" both with God and man. With the death of her husband, she now finds herself in a position to remarry, if she should so choose. Paul's advice is that she would probably be much happier if she remained single and devoted her life to serving Christ and others (Paul highly praised such widows in 1 Timothy 5). If, however, she should choose to remarry, Paul attaches only one restriction: she should marry "only in the Lord."

Although countless theories as to the meaning of this phrase have been advocated over the years, most scholars believe it signifies the widow was to marry only a fellow believer. If so, this would be yet another occasion where the IDEAL of the Creator was being upheld as the divine standard for marriage. Ideally, a couple would not only share a marital covenant with one another, but a spiritual covenant with their Lord — "being heirs together of the grace of life" [1 Peter 3:7, *King James Version*].

For men and women to leave God out of their interpersonal relationships, and especially for them to leave Him out of their marriages, is a serious mistake that invariably proves to be costly. IDEAL marriage is an intimate interpersonal relationship the totality of which is governed by the principles of the Lord, and the participants of which, as one flesh, devote themselves body, soul and spirit unto Him. For a committed believer to enter into a covenant of marriage with one *not* so devoted to God and His will for their lives, is to place this union in jeopardy from the very beginning.

In the time of the apostle Paul, for a believing woman to place herself under the dominion of a non-believer was an act of extreme spiritual foolhardiness. Life for a woman in the first century, who was striving to maintain her devotion to the Lord, was difficult enough under the best of circumstances without intentionally placing herself in submission to an unbelieving husband. Paul calls these widows, and, in principle, all believers, to consider a life-long covenant of marriage *only* with those who will share their spiritual journey, and who will walk together with them toward the goal of eternal life.

THE PASTORAL EPISTLES

The only remaining statements by the apostle Paul relevant to the subject of divorce and remarriage are contained within the pages of the Pastoral Epistles; specifically, within those sections enumerating the qualities and qualifications for spiritual leadership in the Lord's church. Because 1 & 2 Timothy and Titus were written to individual church leaders, rather than to entire congregations, and deal heavily with the life, practice, organization, leadership, and discipline of the church, Paul Anton, in the year 1726, referred to them collectively as the "Pastoral Epistles," a name which has remained until this day. They are letters of encouragement and guidance from an older pastor (Paul) who sought perhaps to groom these two younger evangelists (Timothy and Titus) for many additional years of effective leadership to the church.

Paul penned these epistles in the final years of his life. The first epistle to Timothy was written from the region of Macedonia, possibly from the city of Philippi, about midway through the year 63 A.D. It was sent to the city of Ephesus where Timothy was serving as an evangelist. A few months later, in the fall of 63 A.D., Paul, who was likely in the city of Corinth at the time, wrote a letter to Titus, who was laboring for the Lord on the island of Crete. As the year 66 A.D. drew to a close, Paul found himself in a prison cell in Rome under the sentence of death. Just weeks before being beheaded by direction of the evil Emperor Nero, early in 67 A.D., Paul wrote one last letter: a moving, inspirational message to Timothy in Ephesus. These three pastoral epistles are among the most tender and personal of all Paul's writings.

It is within the first two pastoral letters, however, that Paul speaks to the issue before us, and he does so within the context of a matter he deemed to be of tremendous importance to the life of the church: the qualities which were to be exemplified in the lives of its spiritual leaders. Among the many qualities which are discussed, there is one (mentioned twice in connection with elders; once with reference to deacons) which is crucial to one's understanding of Paul's teaching on the matter of divorce and remarriage (although neither term is specifically mentioned). The spiritual leaders of the church are to be "the husband of but one wife" [1 Timothy 3:2,12; Titus 1:6].

In the original Greek text this statement would more literally be rendered, "a one woman man" or "a man of one woman." It refers to an attitude of heart; an inner portrait of one who is deeply committed to just one woman. Although the world abounds with men given over to the desires of the flesh, whose eyes never cease roving and whose lustful appetites never seem sated, such attitudes and actions must be foreign to the heart of God's leaders.

Genuine pastors of God's flock understand the importance of leading by example [1 Peter 5:3]. They perceive the significance, to both themselves and their followers, of a singleness of commitment to the covenants established with their God and their spouses. Their lives are to be a reflection of God's IDEAL; the Creator's original design for marriage: one man committed to one woman for life. In attitude and action the true leader of God's people is a one woman man!

It should be noted that Paul was giving this direction in the context of a period of time, and within a society, both religious and secular, where marriage had become increasingly trivialized and cheapened. The IDEAL of God was all but forgotten by mankind. The practice of polygamy was rampant, as was the heartless abuse and abandonment of wives. Men were living lives of reckless wantonness; utterly consumed with their own lusts; focused entirely upon the pursuit of their own self-interests. The concept of marriage as a *covenant* meant nothing; honor and commitment were mocked; women were regarded as little more than possessions to be obtained or discarded on a whim. And, to the horror of society, women were beginning to step out of their "assigned place" to follow the horrendous example of the men. It was a time of moral and spiritual chaos; a time in which strong spiritual leadership was desperately needed.

Those who were called to stand before the people of God and guide them in the paths of righteousness, must of necessity have a far better comprehension of the mind of God than those about them. They must perceive the beauty and value of godly living. They must know the Creator's design for every area of their lives, and must further be actively seeking to achieve these IDEALS. Godly leaders must be able to demonstrate, through the example of their own daily living, as well as through their teaching, that God's IDEALS are not only understandable, but attainable — even preferable! God has always required an extra measure of maturity, wisdom, and spirituality from His leaders so that they might genuinely prove to be "examples to the flock" [1 Peter 5:3]. "Remember your leaders who have spoken God's message to you; and as you observe their manner of life, imitate their faith" [Hebrews 13:7].

A leader in the church who was a polygamist, for instance, would be a very poor example to the flock of the Creator's original intent for marriage. His life would be a public declaration that he had no real understanding of or appreciation for God's IDEAL. A great many biblical scholars, incidentally, are convinced this is the true significance of the phrase "one woman man." Spiritual leaders in the church, they declare, are to be monogamous, both in heart and practice, rather than polygamous. A few translations of the Scriptures even go so far as to state, in 1 Timothy 3:12, that spiritual leaders must be chosen from among those men "who have not been polygamous."

There seems to be little question, however, that Paul's characterization of the heart of God's spiritual leader does not stop with a mere abhorrence of and abstinence from the practice of polygamy. It entails far more than that, although it does indeed include it. One who is genuinely a one woman man will also remain faithful to his wife, and to his covenant with her. Seeking out illicit sexual relationships would be unthinkable to him. One will never observe him letting his eyes gaze lustfully and longingly upon another woman, thus committing adultery with her in his heart. He is a "one woman man." His heart is devoted entirely to the only woman in his life: his wife!

Seeking to terminate his covenant of marriage with his spouse when the problems common to all marital relationships occur in his own marriage will be the farthest thing from his mind. "Divorce" is not a part of his vocabulary! Challenges to the relationship will be worked out and overcome; sacrifices will be made; humility, patience, forbearance and love will be practiced. The sailing may not always be smooth, but abandoning ship is not viewed as a viable option.

CASE HISTORY — *Marvin and Gail had been joined in marriage for 45 years when she died of cancer. They were the parents of three children, all of whom had grown into responsible Christian men and women. Marvin had served as a spiritual leader in his church for ten years at the time of Gail's death. Two weeks after her funeral, a committee of members informed Marvin he must resign as one of the congregation's leaders, for he was no longer the "husband of one wife" — he was now the husband of no wife, thus unfit to continue serving as a spiritual guide for the church. Marvin was deeply hurt, but to keep peace in the congregation, he resigned his position of leadership.*

Were the church members correct in their interpretation of this passage from the Pastoral Epistles? Were they justified in requiring Marvin to step down as one of their spiritual leaders? By carefully examining the intent of the apostle Paul in giving these various qualities of leadership, and becoming aware of the true purpose of the "one woman man" principle, one will quickly see the interpretation of the committee of members was completely erroneous.

Paul was not giving a legalistic check list, but providing insight into the nature of a godly leader's heart. Among other things, a spiritual leader will possess the quality of being a one woman man. It is the nature of his heart; he is lovingly and faithfully committed to his spouse. This was no less true of Marvin *after* Gail's death than it was *before*. He possessed a quality of heart that demonstrated itself in genuine, undistracted devotion to another. For 45 years he successfully displayed his commitment to the IDEAL; a commitment to a divine principle which her death did not make void. He was, and continues to be, a man whose heart is filled with an appreciation of the beauty of the

Creator's original design for marriage. He lived it, and continues to proclaim it. Indeed, his devotion to this divine principle is stronger now than ever before, for he experienced first-hand the blessings of achieving God's IDEAL for marriage. Marvin is able to bring to his flock the wisdom, experience and example of 45 years of successful marriage. Marvin was, and is, and always will be a one woman man; it is a quality of his heart. The fact of his wife's death in no way negates this quality of heart. Thus, there is no just cause why he should relinquish his position as a spiritual leader.

Suppose Marvin decides at some point in the future to marry again, and spends the remainder of his life in a loving, faithful relationship with Janet, his new spouse? Would this disqualify him from serving as a spiritual leader? Would he now be considered a *"two* woman man?"* If Paul's intent in his discussion of leadership qualities was to provide a legalistic and numeric check list, then perhaps the answer would be "Yes." But Paul, legalism's greatest opponent, was not counting wives; rather, he was calling the church to consider the nature of a man's *heart.* Is Marvin still a "one woman man" in his heart? Absolutely! He is entirely devoted to his covenant with Janet, and he spends the remainder of his life living the IDEAL with her. Being a one woman man is an *attitude of heart* that manifests itself in the actions of one's life. In no way was Marvin ever inconsistent with that attitude or those actions. He was by nature and desire a one woman man, and the fact that death claimed his first wife and he later entered into a covenant with a second, neither diminished nor negated this marvelous quality of heart.

> CASE HISTORY — *Frank and Ruby married one another right after graduating from high school. They had dated through their junior & senior years; everyone knew they were "meant for each other." For the first five years things went well. Frank was completely devoted to Ruby; she was the center of his universe; the focus of his life. In his eyes, no other woman existed. He was truly a one woman man. But, Frank's world collapsed unexpectedly one day when Ruby informed him she had met a man where she worked with whom she would rather spend her life.*

DOWN, BUT NOT OUT

He had asked her to come away with him, and she had accepted. She claimed she still loved Frank very much; that he had always been a good and devoted husband; this was something she "just had to do."

Ruby filed for divorce, in spite of Frank's pleas that they seek help to save their marriage. She freely admitted this was her decision and that Frank was in no way to blame for the breakdown of the relationship. Frank was devastated, spending the next twelve years alone, trying as best he could to continue on with his life; hoping Ruby would come back. Seeking out another relationship was the farthest thing from his mind; Ruby had been the only woman for him; he couldn't imagine being with anyone else.

One day, at a church function, Frank was introduced to Caroline. She began showing an interest in him, and slowly Frank began to emerge from the depths of his lengthy despair. Two years later, at the age of 37, Frank married Caroline, a 30 year old school teacher who had never married. For the next 25 years they enjoyed a warm, loving relationship; one in which both were completely devoted to the other. They had two sons, both of whom accepted Christ and actively served Him.

When Frank was 62 years old, the congregation where he worshipped began a search for additional spiritual leaders. The members repeatedly submitted his name for consideration, but the current leaders refused to call him to serve. His first wife had left him, and he had remarried. Thus, he was not, they ruled, the "husband of one wife."

Were these leaders right in forbidding Frank to serve the congregation as a spiritual leader? Again, how one responds will depend largely on how one interprets the phrase "one woman man." Is it a legal mandate, denoting *quantity*? Or, is it the focus of one's heart and life, denoting *quality*? If one opts for the former, he will probably agree with the view that Frank is disqualified; if one opts for the latter, he likely will disagree with that assessment.

The tragic fact that Ruby chose to abandon Frank and pursue her own selfish interests in no way negated Frank's commitment to God's IDEAL. If anything, it strengthened that commitment, for Frank had experienced first-hand the agony that ensues from a failure to achieve it. Frank had been sinned against; he was a victim; adultery had been committed *against* him, not *by* him. According to the teaching of Jesus, he was guilty of nothing. Throughout his marriage to Caroline the nature of his heart never changed; he was true to her, just as he had been to Ruby. He was a "one woman man," an attitude of heart which he consistently demonstrated in his life.

Had the situation been reversed, however; had it been Frank who abandoned Ruby so he could run off with Caroline; things would be much different. Even though he and Caroline may have established a warm, loving relationship, and raised their children well, and become respected members of their community and church, Frank will always have that experience in his past where he "dealt treacherously" with the wife of his youth, his companion by covenant [Malachi 2]. This is not to suggest that God will not forgive Frank, if genuine repentance has occurred in his heart, but such behavior *does* incur consequences. *One* such consequence is that by his past failure to display a "one woman man" quality of heart, he has forfeited the right to serve as a spiritual leader in the church.

God has called His spiritual leaders to be living *examples* to the flock. Their lives must be models of successful living. When men, women and young people look to their leaders, they must be able to clearly see, from the pattern of their lives, that God's IDEAL is both attainable and maintainable. The leader's heart must be attuned with God's, and their lives consistently lived in keeping with His will, if they would be effective *guides* for their flock.

When the marriage of a godly leader is ended by the death of his spouse, this in no way voids that *quality of heart* that is, and always was, focused upon the IDEAL; he remains a one woman man. When a faithless wife abandons her husband, breaking their covenant of marriage, this also, in itself, does not void that quality of heart necessary for spiritual leadership. Remember, God's wife left Him, and in so doing did not diminish His character in the least. Even should this man remarry, as did God, that in no way suggests his heart is any less committed to the IDEAL; he is still, and always was, a one woman man. Indeed, should either of these men serve as spiritual leaders, they can demonstrate through their lives how the one woman man remains faithful to the IDEAL even in the face of such challenges as the death of a spouse or her unfaithfulness to him.

A man who has dealt treacherously with his wife, however; who has displayed a total disregard for the Creator's original design for marriage; who has cast aside the IDEAL; simply *cannot* lift up his life as an example of consistent godly living. Spiritual leaders are to be living *success* stories; living testimonies to the validity of God's design; a walking, talking, flesh-and-blood illustration that the Creator's original intent for marriage *can* be achieved. Those who have failed in this respect are simply incapable of providing such an example. This is not to suggest they are not fully forgiven, or that they can't effectively serve in other areas, but they have forever forfeited, as a consequence of their previous treachery, the ability to be a living *example* to the flock of God's IDEAL for marriage.

This concludes the teaching of the apostle Paul with regard to the subject of divorce and remarriage. He makes no further mention of it in any of his many writings. This also concludes the testimony of Scripture, as contained in both the Old and New Covenant documents. The totality of what the Lord has chosen to reveal to mankind on this issue is preserved in these few passages. One's theology, to be truly Scriptural, must be formulated from no other source than these alone.

All that remains in this study is to draw some practical conclusions as to the overall teaching of the Bible with respect to divorce and remarriage, and to offer some helpful, healing insights from God's Word to those who are down, but not yet out.

Chapter 8
Healing Grace: A Message of Hope

Ours is a society in which an alarming number of one's fellow life-travelers are suffering the trauma of marital breakdown. To compound the tragedy, this pain is often endured alone. The very ones to whom the hurting should be able to turn for help and healing, the people of God, are far too frequently the very ones driving them deeper into despair. A self-righteous dogmatism, generated by a woeful misunderstanding and misapplication of the Scriptures, has all but buried God's grace from view. The legalistic wrangling of the religious over the subject of divorce and remarriage has resulted in far more heartache than healing.

It is time for the fuming factions within the family of God to put aside their weapons of warfare, and begin tending to the wounded which lie all about them on the battlefield of life. While scholastics verbally assault one another over matters of opinion largely drawn from unnecessary inferences, implications, or outright manipulations of the biblical text, families are being fractured. It is time for the people of God to become ministers of healing and heralds of hope. The time has come for us to begin applying the healing salve of God's grace.

God has not called His children to be judges, jurors and executioners of those who have suffered the vicious afflictions of the evil one; He has called them to be restorers and reclaimers of those who are down, but not yet out. The devoted disciple must lift the burdens from the backs of his fellow men, not impose additional ones; assist the downtrodden to their feet, not trample them underfoot.

To contribute to the accomplishment of this godly goal, one must bear God's gracious message to five distinct groups, each of whom are intimately involved in the issue before us in this study:

1. Those responsible for dealing treacherously with their mates and breaking their covenant of marriage with them.

2. Those forced to initiate a divorce against a spouse who, by their faithless attitudes and actions, have destroyed the marital relationship.

3. The divorced spouse who remarries, and those who marry them.

4. Those who have been victimized by the actions of a treacherous mate.

5. The members of the Lord's church, to whom God has bestowed a sacred trust.

Unto each of these groups, God, in His Word, has revealed a message of grace and issued a call to action. It is imperative that this message be clearly perceived and proclaimed by His people, for, if embraced, it will facilitate the much needed healing of those who are down, but not out.

A MESSAGE TO COVENANT BREAKERS

To those who have willfully broken their covenants of marriage with their spouses, and who have dealt treacherously with their mates, God's message is: they have sinned! They are responsible for creating a situation which God declares to be abhorrent in His sight. "'I hate divorce,' says the Lord God of Israel" [Malachi 2:16]. God declares Himself a witness to this act of broken faith with one's covenant partner [Malachi 2:14], and further declares those guilty of such treachery as being devoid of even a "remnant of the Spirit" [Malachi 2:15]. The Son of God charges such ones with the sin of adultery, for they have, by their faithless actions and attitudes, destroyed a sacred union created and established by God. Such guilt carries with it severe consequences. Not only have these individuals inflicted tremendous pain upon others, but they have rendered themselves unfit to inherit the kingdom of God [1 Corinthians 6:9-10].

Undoubtedly, such individuals will seek to justify their actions as best they can with friends and loved ones. The Pharisees certainly tried, but the Lord was not deceived. Jesus rebuked them, saying, "You are the ones who justify yourselves in the eyes of men, but God knows your hearts" [Luke 16:15]. Abraham Lincoln once stated, "It is true that you may fool all the people some of the time; you can even fool some of the people all the time; but you can't fool all of the people all the time." To this observation one might add: "And you can never fool God any time!" Paul makes it quite clear that God will not be played for a fool, and that a man will reap exactly what he sows [Galatians 6:7]. This is the principle of reciprocity. Regardless of their efforts to justify themselves, those who have dealt treacherously with their spouses will reap a harvest of divine retribution. "For judgment will be merciless to one who has shown no mercy" [James 2:13].

Needless to say, such a willful covenant breaker is not in an enviable position from a spiritual and eternal point of view. "But in spite of this, there is still hope!" These were the words of Shecaniah to Ezra, as recorded in Ezra 10:2. Following the Babylonian captivity, some of the men among God's chosen people began violating their covenants with their Jewish wives, casting them aside in favor of the foreign women from neighboring nations. They had been unfaithful to their mates and to their Maker. Their situation was serious — but not hopeless!

God is a merciful God; a gracious God; "not wanting anyone to perish, but everyone to come to repentance" [2 Peter 3:9]. The Lord declares only one sin to be unforgivable: blasphemy against the Holy Spirit [Matthew 12:31-32]. Thus, "there is still hope," says Shecaniah, for the covenant breaker (the adulterer) if they will genuinely repent and turn to God for healing and restoration.

This means they must acknowledge the wrongful nature of their behavior; a confession generated by the realization that they have failed their spouse and their God, and by a deep, heartfelt sense of guilt for these hurtful actions. With contrition comes redirection; a refocusing upon God's will. With redirection comes rededication. One must completely renounce the behavior of the past that brought so much pain and misery to others, and become devoted to striving for God's IDEAL in all areas of life. In the words of John to the people of his day,

"Produce fruit in keeping with repentance" [Luke 3:8].

Part of the fruit of a penitent heart will be to seek the forgiveness of the spouse one betrayed and put away. If not too late, one should also strive for a reconciliation [1 Corinthians 7:11]. God's will is that, if possible, the relationship be restored; the covenant re-established; the wounds healed. Realistically, however, reconciliation is not always possible. Too much time may have elapsed; new marital unions may have been entered. It's also possible the spouse with whom one dealt treacherously may never be willing to forgive or forget; the wounds may be too deep.

If one's efforts to reconcile have been met with absolute rejection, then move on with life, living it from that moment forward in complete submission to the will of God. As Jesus told the woman caught in the act of adultery, "Go now and leave your life of sin" [John 8:11]. He refused to condemn her, but rather challenged her to a life of faithfulness from then on. Such is the nature of our Lord's love and grace. Therefore, develop a strong personal relationship with the Lord and His people, serve Him faithfully, and seek to instill the lessons learned the hard way in the hearts of others.

Should such covenant breakers, transformed by the grace of God, choose to marry again at some point in the future, there is nothing in Scripture which would forbid them from doing so. God's message to them is: don't repeat the mistakes of the past; be faithful to your covenant of marriage; strive with all of your being to achieve the IDEAL.

A MESSAGE TO THOSE FORCED TO INITIATE DIVORCE

Many times a spouse will be forced to initiate a divorce against their mate when they themselves do not truly desire the breakdown of the relationship. If a husband is continually engaging in illicit sexual encounters with others, for example, and refuses to cease his immoral behavior, the wife may have no choice but to legally terminate this emotional abuse to which she is being subjected by her faithless husband. Although it is true that she is the one who initiated the divorce against him, nevertheless it is *he* who must bear the responsibility and culpability for the dissolution of the covenant of marriage. As noted earlier in this study, this is the significance of the Lord's so-called "exception clause" which is recorded in the writings of Matthew.

To individuals who find themselves in such situations, the Lord has a consoling message of grace: although they did indeed initiate the divorce against their mate, they are guilty of nothing. Because of the unfaithfulness of their spouse to the covenant of marriage, they have become victims. They have not sinned, but rather have been sinned against; they have not committed adultery by securing a divorce, rather adultery has been committed against them because the covenant was destroyed against their will by the devious actions of their spouse.

Although this certainly does not lessen the pain and trauma of one's failed marriage, perhaps this realization of guiltlessness before God will at least bring a certain sense of inner calm. Among the first questions asked of spiritual counselors by those involved in the termination of a covenant of marriage are, "Was this divorce Scriptural? Is God upset with me? Have I sinned?" These are questions that greatly concern the spouse who seeks to live in accordance with God's will, but who is now having to face life with the reality of having experienced a destroyed marital covenant. Not knowing how one's standing with God will be affected by this disunion can lead to increased anxiety and intensified distress. How these concerns are addressed by those who seek to counsel them will have a tremendous impact upon the extent of their healing and ultimate recovery physically, emotionally, and spiritually.

Far too many spiritual guides within the religious world, through a misunderstanding of Jesus Christ's "exception clause," and the full meaning, semantic range, and application of such words as "porneia" and "moicheia," have mistakenly conveyed to countless people that the only divorce God will sanction is the one secured because of the sexual infidelity of a spouse. Such a view has resulted in all *other* causes for divorce being labeled "Unscriptural." Such a narrow theology allows its adherents to make "easy judgments" as to another's acceptability to

175

God and His church, and, if one is deemed "unworthy," various forms of shunning are sure to follow.

This erroneous theological stance has not only led to unnecessary pain, but to some of the most unbelievable manipulative efforts imaginable by those poor souls desperate to maintain their "good standing" within the church. There have been several cases, for example, where women who were being physically and emotionally abused by their husbands actually hired prostitutes to seduce their mates, so that when they walked in on them in the midst of their act of "committing adultery," they would have "Scriptural grounds" for divorcing them. What a tragedy that some have felt so entrapped by these harsh human decrees against them that they resorted to such desperate, devious, demeaning measures in an attempt to placate their legalistic leaders.

Is sexual infidelity really the worst abuse one spouse can inflict upon another? Is it truly the *only* sin that can effectively destroy one's covenant relationship? There is no question but what it is a serious violation of trust, and emotionally painful to the spouse who has been betrayed. It most definitely can destroy one's marriage, if repentance and reconciliation are not immediately sought. However, it is far from being the only abusive, treacherous, covenant breaking action one can commit against a mate. Without a doubt, there are acts of unfaithfulness to one's covenant, which are *not* of a sexual nature, far more deplorable, distressful, and destructive.

There are numerous women whose husbands have remained sexually faithful to them, but who are being victimized by these "faithful" husbands through repeated acts of extreme physical and emotional abuse. A significant number of women have been so frequently and severely battered by their husbands over the years that society has established shelters where they may find safe haven. These women have endured not only broken bones, but also broken dreams and broken promises. Their lives have been shattered and their spirits quenched, and a far greater number of them than one would like to admit end up losing their lives at the hands of their husbands.

For anyone to promote the view that God *requires* spouses to remain in such conditions as long as their depraved mate has not actually had sex with another is aberrant and abhorrent! In such circumstances the covenant of marriage has long since been violated and voided. The two may indeed co-exist in the same house, but they do so more as abuser and victim, than as husband and wife.

> CASE HISTORY — *Lisa and Karl had been joined together in marriage for fifteen years. During that time Lisa had been admitted to the hospital six times as a result of the severe beatings she had received from Karl. He was not interested in a sexual relationship with another woman; he had remained faithful to Lisa in that respect. They had tried marital counseling, and he had even gone through anger management classes. All to no avail.*
>
> *One evening the police were called to their house (Karl had been arrested numerous times for spousal abuse and disturbing the peace). Karl was holding a gun to Lisa's head, threatening to kill her. They talked him into releasing her, and then took him to jail. Soon, however, he was back with Lisa. She had considered divorcing him years earlier, but had been told by her Minister that since Karl had not been "unfaithful" to her (i.e., since he hadn't had sex with another woman), she would go to hell if she divorced him. She could live apart from him, but would have to remain celibate for life. No matter how difficult her situation, unless Karl "committed fornication," she must remain married to him. Three months later the police were again called to their home. Karl had beaten Lisa to death.*

Was the advice of the Minister to Lisa correct? Was such advice "Scriptural?" No! Far from it! Sadly, though, such counsel as that which was provided Lisa is dispensed all too frequently by woefully misguided and misinformed counselors. By what twisted rationale does one portray our gracious, loving, merciful God as the type of Being who would condemn to hell a woman who sought release from years of abuse at the hands of her godless spouse?! By understanding "moicheia" as "sexual infidelity only," some have arrived at a distorted, heartless theology that has served only to inflict untold additional suffering upon those already experiencing one of life's greatest traumas. Any theology which *hurts* more than it *heals*; which drives away more than it draws near; should be immediately suspect. If one's view of divorce and remarriage excludes more than it includes; if it labels others as inferior; if it denies certain forgiven sinners the blessings bestowed upon other groups of forgiven sinners; that view is in need of re-examination in light of God's Word.

"Is my divorce Scriptural? Will God condemn me?" When covenants of marriage are dissolved, the question to which God will demand an answer is: who was responsible? It is *that* spouse who must bear the guilt and, ultimately, the consequences of the broken covenant of marriage. If a husband, for example, destroys the covenant of marriage with his wife by his ungodly behavior, whether that behavior was sexual or not, *he* is the guilty party. Even if the wife is the one who actually initiates the divorce against him, it is *she* who has been sinned *against.* The husband, by breaking covenant, has committed "moicheia" against his wife. Will God condemn such a woman? Absolutely not!

One final word to those who have had to divorce their faithless spouse: although you undoubtedly have been deeply hurt by the treachery enacted against you, and which led you to the point of divorcing your mate, don't respond in kind! Remember the attitude of Joseph as he was faced with the prospect of having to divorce Mary, whom he believed to have violated their covenant. Although he could have made a public spectacle of her, shamed and defamed her before the world, even had her executed; even though Joseph was obviously deeply hurt and feeling betrayed; he refused to inflict the same pain upon Mary that she had inflicted, seemingly, upon him!

Although one may have absolutely no option, given their circumstances, but to divorce a godless mate, one *does* have a choice with regard to the attitude he or she displays. This is an opportunity to demonstrate a righteous demeanor; a godly heart. Don't allow yourself to be reduced to the level of the one who afflicted hurt upon you! Instead, let the grace of God shine through your actions and attitudes, so that others will witness the healing power of God working in a life surrendered to His will.

A MESSAGE TO THOSE CONTEMPLATING REMARRIAGE

To those who have experienced a divorce in their past, and are now either in another covenant of marriage, or contemplating one; and to those who either are, or are about to be, married to one who has been divorced; God has a message for you: your union is a legitimate marriage! Although some in the religious world staunchly deny this, and characterize all future relationships as sinful and adulterous, there is simply no Scriptural basis for such an uncharitable position.

When Jesus Christ spoke of the divorced entering into subsequent unions, He spoke of them as "marriages." Paul declared unto the divorced, "If you *do* marry, you have *not* sinned" [1 Corinthians 7:28]. To deny legitimacy to the marriages of those who have been divorced is to deny the teaching of Jesus; to declare them sinful is to contradict the teaching of Paul; to condemn the remarried is to condemn God (who turned to Israel's sister Judah after having divorced the former).

Some, misunderstanding the teachings of God's Word, attempt to bind a state of perpetual celibacy upon the divorced. Others, perhaps feeling more "gracious," seek to bind such a state only upon the guilty spouse. The Scriptures do not endorse either view! "The Lord God said, 'It is not good for the man to be alone'" [Genesis 2:18]. One will not find the addition: "Unless they are divorced." Paul wrote, "Each man should have his own wife, and each woman her own husband" [1 Corinthians 7:2]. Several verses later he commanded those who could not control their sexual appetites to marry, "for it is better to marry than to burn with passion" [vs. 9]. Again, one will find no conditional clause in the text which excludes the divorced from the intent of these principles and commands.

Others teach that the words of Jesus are unmistakable: when the divorced remarry, they "commit adultery," as do those who enter into marriage with them. As previously noted, however, this is *not* what these passages teach. The use of the *passive* voice clearly demonstrates the people of whom Jesus spoke were not committing sin, but rather were being sinned against. They themselves were guilty of nothing. Nowhere in the inspired Scriptures does God forbid a second union to those who have experienced the breakdown of the first. And nowhere are such subsequent unions portrayed as anything other than legitimate covenants of marriage. The characterization "sinful" is of man, not of God.

CASE HISTORY — *Joe, having just been promoted at work, was moved by his company to a new state. He and Denise had been married for fifteen years, and were the proud parents of three sons, all of whom were still living at home. Upon relocating, they immediately affiliated themselves with a local church and became active in the Lord's work in their area.*

One day it came to the attention of the church leaders that Joe had been divorced twenty years earlier, and that Denise was actually his second wife. The leaders met to discuss this "critical problem." They agreed that since man cannot separate what God had joined, Joe's first marriage was still in force, and his second union was an adulterous affair. Their decision was that this couple must terminate their sinful relationship immediately.

Their main problem, however, was what to do about the children of this second union. After much debate they concluded the following: since it was their belief that adultery was strictly an act of sexual intercourse with a person other than one's spouse, Joe and Denise would be allowed to live together for the purpose of caring for the children as long as they slept in separate rooms and ended their sexual relationship. In this way they could avoid "committing adultery."

To appease their religious leaders, and to keep their family together, and because they had been led to believe they would be eternally lost to do otherwise, Joe and Denise agreed to these terms. Thus, they lived together … apart.

Although this example may seem rather bizarre, the reader should be aware that it is an actual case which occurred a few years ago (although the names have obviously been changed). These are real people, enduring real acts of abuse in the name of a "sound doctrine" that is outrageous and perverted. These are acts imposed by a legalistic leadership totally devoid of even a basic understanding of the teachings of the Lord with regard to this issue. How pitifully the people of God are often treated by those who fail to perceive God's wondrous message of grace and healing! Shockingly, the above actual case has been repeated hundreds, perhaps even thousands, of times in churches led by men who are guilty of militant ignorance.

What the above leaders have failed to realize is that they themselves are far more guilty of adultery than Joe and Denise! "Moicheia" signifies the disruption and breakdown of a covenant of marriage. In this case, who must bear the guilt for destroying the marriage of Joe and Denise? It's ironic, is it not, that these misguided church leaders, in their efforts to be "Scriptural," have actually violated the very passages they ignorantly sought to enforce, and in so doing became the "adulterers" (covenant breakers) themselves!

God has called all men to the joys of IDEAL marriage. Many, perhaps through their own fault, or due to the treachery of their mate, have failed to achieve that goal. They have experienced a divorce; a tragic unraveling of what should have been one of God's greatest blessings for their life. The determination of who must ultimately bear the responsibility, guilt, and consequences for that disunion rests in the hands of God — a *forgiving* God, one might add, if genuine repentance occurs and forgiveness is sought. A past failure to achieve the IDEAL does not disqualify one from seeking after it in the future. To the woman caught in the very act of sexual infidelity, Jesus refused to utter a single word of condemnation. Instead, He graciously said, "Go now and leave your life of sin." Paul spoke of "forgetting what is behind and straining toward what is ahead" [Philippians 3:13].

What better advice could one offer the divorced for consideration than this! Leaving the failings of the past behind, and equipped with the knowledge gained from those tragic experiences, move forward in your relationship with God, reaching out for the prize of the IDEAL in your new covenant of marriage.

A MESSAGE TO THE INNOCENT PARTY

A great many people who find themselves in a state of divorce are there through no fault of their own. They are the victims of divorce; the innocent party. By the desire and action of a faithless spouse, a covenant of marriage has been terminated and one formerly loved has been abandoned.

Those who have had this state imposed upon them will experience a wide range of emotions. Shock, anguish, emptiness, confusion, depression, despair, anger, self-pity, hopelessness, alienation, low self-esteem, resignation, regrets, and recriminations are just a few of the numerous feelings with which the divorced typically struggle. It should be noted, however, that a point in time will come in which these various negative emotions begin to give way to a more positive perspective. Relief, optimism, acceptance, a new sense of self-worth, and perhaps even a certain amount of excitement about the future develop within the healing heart.

It is extremely important, with respect to one's ultimate healing, that the negative emotions, which seem to overwhelm the victim during the early stages of a failed marriage, *not* be denied or suppressed. Such feelings are natural, and must be worked through as a part of the healing process. Some are able to accomplish this with a minimum of outside assistance; others require more aid from supportive friends, loved ones, and even professionals to effectively work through certain emotions.

It is essential that one not become fixated, or "stuck," in any one stage of the emotional healing process. Those unable to move beyond the anger stage, for example, have been known to reach a point where they actually inflicted great harm, and even death, upon their former spouse. Others, unable to work through their sense of hopelessness and despair, have at times taken their own lives. Rather than allowing such extremes to be reached, one should seek out help if experiencing difficulty moving beyond a particular emotional stage. Various professionals, both secular and spiritual, numerous support groups, friends and family are all there to provide a helping hand — one should not hesitate to avail themselves of such assistance in time of need.

Another strong emotion the put-away spouse often feels is self-recrimination. Blaming themselves for the fact that their husband or wife divorced them is common. "It must have been my fault! If only I had done ... Or, if only I had not done ... ." Hindsight is said to be 20/20. In retrospect, one can usually detect areas in which something might have been said or done differently. However, one cannot relive the past; it is finished. One can learn from the experiences of the past; perhaps even make restitution for one's errors; certainly be forgiven if repentance is sought; but to repair the past, so as to alter the present and future, is beyond the realm of possibility.

For emotional healing to take place, and for one to begin to move forward into a bright new future, it is imperative that forgiveness be perceived and put into practice. The spouse who has been divorced by a faithless mate has been sinned against; their former spouse has broken faith with them, and in so doing has robbed them of something very precious: a sacred covenant of marriage and the hope of experiencing the IDEAL through that relationship. It would be easy to harbor feelings of resentment, bitterness, anger and hatred, but such emotions will ultimately do more harm to the one who bears them, than to the one against whom they are directed.

The pathway to healing is paved with forgiveness. One must turn the hurt and bitterness over to God. Regardless of the nature or intensity of the grievance against oneself, forgiveness must be practiced [Colossians 3:13]. If punishment needs to be meted out for the afflictions experienced, God will handle it. "Do not take revenge, my friends, but leave room for God's wrath, for it is written: 'It is mine to avenge; I will repay,' says the Lord" [Romans 12:19].

If there are children involved, and in a great many cases there are, the divorced spouse must be extremely careful not to pass on to them the hurt, frustration and anger they may be feeling against their mate. The children will be experiencing enough suffering of their own; they don't need to be utilized as pawns by embittered, battling parents. In such cases, the ones who experience the greatest loss as a result of the divorce are the children! Difficult though it may be to accomplish, display a godly attitude throughout the ordeal. The results of such behavior, both to oneself and to one's children, will be well worth the effort.

As the Lord died upon the cross He forgave those who mocked, cursed, battered and killed Him. The injury inflicted upon Him was wrongful; He was innocent — yet, He forgave! The victim of a faithless spouse has also been made to suffer wrongfully; they are innocent. Nevertheless, the high road is to follow the example of Jesus Christ. Commend your life into the hands of God — and *forgive*.

Those who are divorced, especially those newly divorced, should be aware that they are in an extremely vulnerable emotional state during this time. The desire for love, acceptance, nurturing, and support is so strong that often they rush headlong into a relationship with the first person who shows any degree of interest in them. These rebound relationships can potentially be more harmful than healing due to many still unresolved emotional issues within the newly divorced individual. The wise course is to give oneself sufficient time to heal before seeking out another relationship. One will be less vulnerable, more emotionally stable, more focused upon one's future course and expectations for life, and more likely to be objective and wise in the selection of one's next mate. Time is a healing element; it should be utilized to the fullest.

To the divorced, a word of advice: be cautious of advice! The divorced will receive great amounts of it, some solicited, some unsolicited; some sound, some unsound; some spiritual, some unspiritual. The vast majority of these advisors will be well-meaning, sincere, godly men and women; but, some will not. Take care that the course of action being presented is one consistent with the teaching of Scripture, and one which ultimately leads to emotional and spiritual healing.

One of the greatest truths which can be conveyed to those who have been the victims of divorce is that God loves them and cares for them. It is staggering the number of individuals who admit they feel themselves to be "put away by God" as a result of having been put away by their former spouse. Sadly, such feelings are often encouraged by misguided church leaders and members who view the divorced as spiritually inferior. Do not confuse their negative perceptions and assessments with God's. God loves the divorced — it is the *state* of divorce that He hates, not those victimized by it. Draw near to God, trust Him, confide in Him, pour out your heart to Him — and healing will come.

The divorced should further realize that they are not alone. Others have successfully survived the breakdown of a covenant of marriage and are now leading happy, fulfilled lives. They have worked through the emotional roller coaster ride one may now be experiencing; they know firsthand the special struggles one faces daily. Seek out these people and secure their assistance. Many of them have formed themselves into recognized support and recovery groups; others are simply caring individuals willing to invest some time in bringing the afflicted into contact with God's healing grace. They will make the journey toward emotional and spiritual wholeness far easier than if one seeks to travel that path alone.

There is a God in heaven who has genuine love and concern for those who are hurting. He also has many compassionate disciples who are willing to help the afflicted experience again the joys of life. Realize also that your experience will one day place you in the unique position of being able to render assistance to another who is experiencing the trauma of marital breakdown. Look upon this time as training for ministry, and realize that God has a place in His kingdom for such ministers of healing. You may be *down*, but you are not *out*!!

A MESSAGE TO THE CHURCH

The final group to whom God extends a vital message with regard to this matter is perhaps the most critical of all to the success of the healing process: the church. This universal body of believers is "the pillar and foundation of the truth" [1 Timothy 3:15], but, has it truly been upholding truth in its teaching concerning divorce and remarriage? The "called out" of God have further been given the responsibility of the "ministry" and the "message of reconciliation" [2 Corinthians 5:18-19], but, has its message been one of reconciliation or alienation? If the church is anything other than a redemptive, healing fellowship, then somewhere along the way it has lost sight of its *mission*. If its proclamation is not one of grace, love, forgiveness, and acceptance, it has lost sight of its *message*.

What specifically are the responsibilities of the church with regard to those experiencing the trauma of divorce and the frequent stigma of remarriage? Consider the following Ten Commandments with which the church should seek to comply in order to promote the healing process, and to possibly prevent such covenant breakdowns in the future:

COMMANDMENT ONE
Thou shalt promote prayerful, in-depth study of God's Word on marriage, divorce and remarriage in every congregation of believers in the One Body.

Before the church can presume to speak intelligently and convincingly for God on *any* subject, it must first be thoroughly acquainted with the entirety of His teaching relevant to that issue. "If anyone speaks, he should do it as one speaking the very words of God" [1 Peter 4:11]. The church must also understand *how to apply* that teaching to the challenges and temptations of daily life. What was God's original intent for marriage? What provisions did He make in the Law of Moses for the heartless actions of men and women as they repeatedly violated that divine intent? What message of grace and healing is extended through the teachings of Jesus Christ and the apostle Paul? The people of God are too often woefully lacking in this area of knowledge, and this deficit of understanding is critical in its negative effects upon those desperately in need of healing.

Before the church can ever effectively promote *healing*, however, it must promote *education*. God's people must *know* God's mind. Without that knowledge, which is gained only through careful, prayerful examination of His revealed Word, the church is ill-equipped to offer the guidance so desperately needed in the world today. Indeed, it will likely only do more harm than good, as has too frequently been the case when ill-informed disciples seek to "minister" to those who are hurting.

As a part of this educational process, a local congregation of believers must insure that all preconceptions and prejudices, all opinions, traditions, and biases drawn from one's religious heritage are set aside in favor of an honest, open, free investigation into God's revealed Truth. *Genuine* Truth has absolutely nothing to fear from such a process; Truth remains Truth regardless of the intensity of the investigation into it. Only one's *misconceptions* and *biases* need fear exposure to the light of God's Word. Entering into such a study with the right attitude will assure that change will be embraced if one's previous position is found to be inconsistent with the teachings of Scripture. May the people of God be honest enough and courageous enough to *change*, even in the face of criticism, when God's Truth is perceived.

COMMANDMENT TWO
Thou shalt take seriously thy obligation to train up thy young people in the knowledge of God's IDEAL for marriage, and the consequences of failing to achieve it.

Although this is very similar to the first commandment, in that it involves education, it is far more specific in focus. The church has a responsibility to its youth that when shirked results in the gravest of consequences. A lost generation can easily develop through a failure to faithfully impart God's teachings.

"Train a child in the way he should go" [Proverbs 22:6] is good advice. The local congregation of believers should insure that its youth, from infancy onward, are exposed constantly to the beauty of God's IDEAL for marriage, both in teaching and in practice. With such training they will be better equipped to resist the temptations of the world to depart from the way in which they should go.

COMMANDMENT THREE

Thou shalt not debate and divide while the distressed lie neglected upon thy doorstep.

It is said that while Nero fiddled, Rome burned. In like manner, while the church debates the numerous personal preferences and practices associated with divorce and remarriage, the divorced and remarried themselves are ignored. Victims are in need of love, not lectures; devotion, not debate. A church divided over the issue of divorce is a church incapable of effectively ministering to the divorced.

Look to the example of Jesus. While the Pharisees debated whether it was right for one to heal on the Sabbath, Jesus healed on the Sabbath. Jesus did not spend months in heated debate over the tedious tenets of their religious tradition; He simply did what was right. He healed. The church spends far too much time *debating*, and far too little time *doing*. The time has come for the people of God to set aside the religious wrangling and begin living up to their calling. It is time to promote a ministry of healing, and to proclaim a message of hope.

COMMANDMENT FOUR

Thou shalt seek ways to render practical assistance to victims of divorce.

A woman who has been put away by a faithless spouse, especially if that woman has children still at home, is probably going to need a great deal of practical assistance to face the challenges of daily existence. She may need to secure employment. Day care for young children may need to be obtained. Managing a budget, or coping with finances, may be unfamiliar territory. The list of possible concerns, many of which may be immediate and critical, is endless.

Such tasks, on top of the stress of the divorce itself, can quickly become overwhelming. The church must be prepared to provide immediate assistance to the victims of divorce who may be temporarily unable to cope with the cares which have suddenly been thrust upon them. Don't wait for their circumstances to become so desperate that they are forced to seek the help of the church — go to them first, and graciously demonstrate the love of Christ in action

COMMANDMENT FIVE
Thou shalt utilize thy members as a resource.

There dwells within virtually every community of believers several members who have experienced divorce and remarriage. Some were victims, some were victimizers; some healed quickly, others struggled through the process. The church in the city of Corinth had within its ranks those who previously had been sexually immoral, idolaters, adulterers, male prostitutes, homosexual offenders, thieves, drunkards, slanderers, and swindlers. However, they had been washed clean, sanctified, and justified by God's grace at work in their lives [1 Corinthians 6:9-11]. Imagine the wealth of wisdom and support such transformed people could provide.

Congregations which utilize these members to reach out to their fellow members in pain, and also to the unbelieving public around them, are wise indeed. Victims of divorce need loving support; they need healing; and what better place to find it than among God's people. By providing this living resource to the general public, as well as to one's own members, a congregation of believers not only extends the parameters of God's ministry of healing, but also opens the door for evangelistic opportunities.

COMMANDMENT SIX
Thou shalt allow the divorced to actively serve in the work and worship of the church.

Although the apostle Paul seems to indicate a man who has previously dealt treacherously with his wife may not serve as a spiritual leader to the people of God, nevertheless the divorced can, and should, be allowed to serve in all other areas of the work and worship of the Lord's church. The Scriptures do not indicate that a divorce renders one a second-class citizen in the kingdom of God, or that it renders one unfit for active service in that kingdom.

Further, it will facilitate the healing process of those experiencing the breakdown of a covenant of marriage if they are kept active and working. And what better type of activity with which to be engaged than service to God and His cause. Thus, the church should not restrict the areas in which these forgiven men and women may labor for their Lord.

COMMANDMENT SEVEN
Thou shalt associate with those who have been divorced and remarried.

Although such a commandment may seem rather strange on the surface, it is a sad fact that many of those who have suffered through a divorce find themselves ostracized by their fellow believers. Perhaps believing they might become defiled by association, some in the church have blatantly refused any form of fellowship with those they deem to be "unclean." Such behavior is unworthy of those who profess to be followers of the Lord.

Jesus constantly kept company with those whom the "religious" of His day felt to be unworthy of their acceptance and association. The Lord refused to allow these self-righteous hypocrites to prevent Him from reaching out to those in need of healing. In so doing, He shocked and shamed the very ones who should have been leading the way in lifting up the fallen. The people of God must not become so righteous in their own sight that they are unwilling to embrace those who are struggling with sin in their lives, or who may be the innocent victims of the sinful actions of others.

COMMANDMENT EIGHT
Thou shalt not place restrictions and burdens upon the divorced and remarried that the Lord God Himself has not.

Where has God authorized His people to ostracize those afflicted with the loss of a covenant relationship? By what authority are they banned from involvement in the work and worship of the church? What Scripture declares them unclean, unsaved, and unworthy of one's fellowship? What declaration of our Lord denies them hope, healing, and the opportunity to strive for the IDEAL again in a future relationship?

The Pharisee who thanked God in prayer that he was superior to adulterers [Luke 18:11] did not receive justification from the Lord. Being far more concerned with the exactness of religious forms and outward appearances than with compassion for the plight of one's fellow man, the Pharisees were repeatedly condemned by Jesus Christ. Their legalistic perspective succeeded only in adding burdens and imposing restrictions upon those already being afflicted and weighed down by "the powers of this dark world" and "the spiritual forces of evil in the heavenly realms" [Ephesians 6:12]. To inflict further abuse, rather than proclaiming a gracious message of hope and healing, is simply to affiliate oneself with the forces of the enemy.

The church is called to ministries of reconciliation and restoration; to be a first-aid station for those wounded and weary from the battles of life. It is to be the pillar and support of truth, not the pillar and support of tradition or personal preference. The church must be a community of believers committed to healing, not hindering; to mercy and compassion, not legalism and ritualism; to lifting burdens, not imposing them. "Carry each other's burdens, and in this way you will fulfill the law of Christ" [Galatians 6:2].

COMMANDMENT NINE
Thou shalt listen, not lecture.

There will be occasions when one who is experiencing the trauma of a marital collapse will seek out someone with whom they can share their burden, and from whom they can seek spiritual guidance and encouragement. At such times some are sorely tempted to begin sharing at length with these "poor souls" the vast treasures of their own insights. Resist this temptation! They don't need a dissertation on the dilemmas of divorce — they're living them! They simply need someone who will care enough to quietly and compassionately hear them out; who will allow them to release perhaps years of unexpressed hurt and frustration.

One of the chief qualities of an effective counselor is the ability to listen. Draw them near with words of assurance and comfort; pray for them and with them; show them the love and grace of God. In short, respond to them as Jesus would. As His ambassadors of grace, we must do no less!

COMMANDMENT TEN

Thou shalt demonstrate in action the love, mercy and grace of God unto those who are divorced and remarried.

If the above qualities are not to be found in the church, then where may the afflicted go to discover them?! The nature of God is to be reflected in the attitudes and actions of His people. God is love — we, therefore, must be a people of love. Jesus is the light of the world — thus, we must push back the gloom and darkness of this world with the light of His life and teachings.

The people of God are in a unique position to offer comfort, compassion, and caring to those who are down, but not yet out. By lifting them to their feet, providing them with a safe haven, and embracing them with the loving acceptance of the Father, the church can set the fallen back on the pathway to healing — and, ultimately, to heaven.

Jesus Christ stated, "You will always have the poor among you" [John 12:8]. This is no less true of the divorced. It is a life situation which demonstrates no evidence of subsiding; indeed, with each passing year the numbers rise. The people of God are daily being challenged by this condition, and the world watches as they respond.

Will the church ignore the situation and hope it goes away? Will they debate it and divide over it, while the cries of the wounded go unheeded? Will they formulate a restrictive theology that keeps the victims of divorce at arm's length? Or, will they respond in love, extend hope, and promote healing? God, in His Word, has clearly portrayed the IDEAL, and has displayed how He responds in those situations where His original intent for marriage has failed to be achieved. His teaching is clear, concise, and consistent; His grace is evident in every passage.

Over the years, the simple teaching of Scripture with reference to marriage, divorce and remarriage, however, has been all but obscured by the construction of a complex system of theology built largely upon the foundation of personal preferences and traditional biases. As a result, the hurting are not being healed, and the despairing are not being given hope.

The purpose of this study has been to lift high for view once again the simple truth of God's Word with respect to marriage, divorce and remarriage. The time has come to dismantle the elaborate, tangled labyrinth of theology constructed by men, and return to the crystal clear message of hope found in Scripture. This book is humbly submitted in the hope it might in some small way assist in effecting that change. It is also presented with the fervent prayer that God may use it to open men's eyes to His matchless love and grace for those who are hurting, and that it may serve to facilitate the healing, and motivate the healers, of those who are *down*, but *not out*!